Barbarians at the Public Libr

D1204940

How Postmodern Consumer Capitalism
Threatens Democracy, Civil Education
and the Public Good

Barbarians at the Gates of the Public Library:

How Postmodern Consumer Capitalism Threatens Democracy, Civil Education and the Public Good

By Ed D'Angelo

Library Juice Press, LLC
Duluth, Minnesota

Library Juice Press, LLC
Duluth Minnesota
http://libraryjuicepress.com/

Copyright 2006 Ed D'Angelo—ed_dangelo@hotmail.com

Printed on acid-free paper

ISBN-10: 0-9778617-1-6
ISBN-13: 978-0-9778617-1-2

Alt. CIP:

D'Angelo, Ed.

Barbarians at the gates of the public library : how postmodern consumer capitalism threatens democracy, civil education and the public
good.—Duluth, Minnesota : Library Juice Press LLC, copyright
2006.

Includes bibliography.
Contents: 1. The crisis of democracy and the public library—2. Democracy and profession of librarianship—3. The reasoning public :
public libraries, democracy and the public good—
4. Education, democracy and the public good—5. Education, edification, entertainment and consumption—6. From ethical liberalism to
economic liberalism—7. Coney Island and the rise of mass entertainment—8. Barbarism and entertainment—9. From citizen to consumer—10. Democracy, the public good and the postmodern information economy—11. Markets, bureaucracies and new economy
management theory—12. Postmodern consumer capitalism and the
public library.

1. Public libraries—History. 2. Libraries and capitalism—History. 3.
Libraries and democracy—History. 4. Democracy—History. 5. Entertainment—History. 6. Librarians—Social responsibility. I. Library
Juice Press. II. Title: How postmodern consumer capitalism threatens
democracy, civil education and the public good.

For my grandmother, Jennie,
whose unconditional love
opened a space in which to wonder

Contents

Preface

The tax-supported U.S. public library was first established in various places in New England in the mid-1800s. As Jesse Shera discussed in his book, *Foundations of the Public Library* (1949), the forces that contributed to the origins of the public library were the presence of sufficient economic resources; the urge for conservation of historical records and scholarly materials; local pride; the growing recognition of the social importance of universal public education; the demand for mechanisms of self-education; vocational needs and the religious environment of the times.

Over the next century (mid-1800s to mid-1900s) libraries were established in hundreds of U.S. communities as a means to provide people with access to the cultural record and to provide the resources to support an enlightened population for participation in the democratic process. The idea of the library as a people's university gradually took hold of the popular imagination. In his plea to extend public library service in 1936 Frank Graham, then president of The University of North Carolina, made the connection between universal library service and democracy, "We will not have democracy in America until we have some such nation-wide mutual aid, some such nation-wide cooperation of federal, state, and county governments in this great job, this great democratic responsibility of making libraries locally accessible not only to the privileged millions, but to the 45,000,000, mainly on the farm, without local access to a public library." (*Bulletin of the American Library Association*, 1936). Close ties of libraries to the adult education community persisted through World War II as has been well-described in Margaret E. Monroe's *Library Adult Education:*

The Biography of an Idea (1963). The ideal of support for the autodidact was in itself a compelling argument for the extension of public library service.

"The library faith"—the belief that public libraries support the democratic process, was first defined by Oliver Garceau, author of *The Public Library in the Political Process* (1949), a volume in the Public Library Inquiry. The signing into law of the Library Services Act in 1956 signified that the public library was viewed as an integral part of life in the United States along with schools and public health. In the decades that followed the nature of the public library's mission and role was examined, revised and ultimately devolved back to the local level through the "planning process" model introduced by the American Library Association in 1980. Because of librarianship's insistence that each community develop its own mission and goals, a broad sweeping raison d'être for the institution—agreed upon by the profession at large—no longer exists. And it is this vacuum that Ed D'Angelo addresses in *Barbarians at the Gates of the Public Library.*

In the twenty-first century public librarians in the United States face four socio-cultural trends. These are people's desire for an institution that provides a sense of place in an increasingly fragmented landscape; the convergence of cultural heritage institutions; broader mandates for free choice learning and literacy; and the citizenry's need for a sustained public sphere. However, it has been difficult for public librarians to deal with service development in light of these trends because governments at all levels have been stalled by parochialism and a narrowing of the zeitgeist during the first years of the century (ca. 2000-2006), a period of repressive single party rule. It is too early to speculate on the damage that has been done to the psyche of librarians because of the compromising required

to accede to federal funding during a period when the
spouse of the president, Mrs. Laura Bush, has made libraries her signature project. The "Laura Bush 21st Century
Librarian Program" has come with a high price-tag. The
profession has given her awards, put her on the cover of
professional journals and generally debased itself. This is in
spite of Mrs. Bush's censorship of poetry and her promotion of values that do not coincide with the values of the
American Library Association.

At this time of distress Ed D'Angelo has written *Barbarians at the Gates of the Public Library*—a *cri de cœur* for librarians and readers to recommit to the public library as
an institution grounded in the national desire to provide
access to the knowledge that will enable true democracy.
D'Angelo's treatise is an impassioned analysis of the threat
of postmodern consumer capitalism to the role of the public library as a vital part of an informed public sphere. In
the United States the public library has been affirmed by
the American Library Association—the world's largest
library organization—as a public good and a fundamental
institution for democratic societies (*ALA Handbook*, 2005-
2006, p.46). Yet as writers like Peter MacDonald have argued, corporate inroads have undercut the purposes and
values of librarianship as practiced today (*Progressive Librarian* 1997).

Ed D'Angelo provides a sharply literate review of the
historical and sociological forces that led to the creation of
the public library. As we move further from the founding
of the nation's institutions such as public health agencies,
schools, or public libraries most people have little connection to the grand ideas that gave them birth. Who today
knows Joseph Goldberger, Catherine Beecher, Albert
Shanker, Reverend Thomas Fountain Blue, or Elizabeth
Putnam Sohier? These essential founders of public health,

education and librarianship are all but unknown to the practitioners of the respective professions. And as we move further from understanding the roots of professions, it is easier for repressive governments to devalue education and the practice of essential public goods.

D'Angelo argues that the shift in general understanding of what comprised a public good paralleled the enlightenment and the idea of progress. He makes good use of John Herman Randall's 1940 volume, *The Making of the Modern Mind*, to argue for equal opportunities through education. In some ways D'Angelo's arguments mirror Nobel Prize winner 1998 Nobel Economics laureate, Amartya Sen, whose theories of development and the enhancement of human capabilities argue for democracy as a universal right.

Yet the idea of progress and the blooming of human capabilities have been suffocated by the United States' general embrace of entertainment over intellectual curiosity. The natural tendency of humans to develop has been trampled by the seductive nature of mass culture. "Coney Island" is an iconic metaphor for the shift toward a mass culture that is developed for profit rather than edification. D'Angelo accords the study of popular culture (cult studs) as reflecting market populism, but astutely notes that the market populism of the 1990s originated in theories of corporate management and "served essentially as a cheerleader and public relations champion for capitalism in its moment of glory."

Tracing the conflict between high and mass culture, D'Angelo demonstrates how the tension between the two has come to resolution through the peculiar justification by cultural studies theorists of mass culture's equation with democracy. Using examples from publishing and mass merchandising of paperbacks and newspapers he characterizes the viciousness of the capitalist controlled marketplace, "Gannet gave its readers what they wanted, at least superficially, but only if they were the readers its advertisers wanted to reach." He places these economic constructs in real space using the shopping mall as a symbol of the destruction of public space and the public sphere. *Barbarians at the Gates of the Public Library* can be read, along with John E. Buschman's *Dismantling the Public Sphere* (2003), as a rigorous enumeration of the effects of economic pressures on the public good that is the public library. These books document a time of portentous threat to civic understanding.

D'Angelo develops a rich argument with plentiful examples that give the reader opportunity to understand the process of corruption of the cultural world by capitalism and business. George Soros emerges as a late 20th century man of action who recognizes what he has wrought and attempts through the Open Society to correct the idolization of money over intellectual and democratic values. The end result of the cult of consumerism is the abandonment of civic education and the loss of the social capacity for civic deliberation.

The public library, an institution founded with the hope of extending universal education throughout the life of citizens, has not been immune to post-liberal consumerism. Since the appointment of George W. Bush to the presidency of the United States, the destruction of public education with the No Child Left Behind Act, and the slashing of college student funding, the United States faces a time when entertainment is much easier to engage than thoughtful contemplation. In my classes in public librarianship I assign *Barbarians at the Gates of the Public Library*. The précis of the history of ideas provided by D'Angelo are a demanding but rewarding first week of class.

If public librarians can re-engage with our foundations of intellectual rigor, commitment to democracy and appreciation for the human record, the gates may be shored up and the barbarians may withdraw. In *Barbarians at the Gates of the Public Library* Ed D'Angelo provides a way for librarians to re-evaluate the menace of a consumption-based society that undermines the democratic purpose of the public library.

Kathleen de la Peña McCook
Distinguished University Professor
School of Library and Information Science
University of South Florida
April, 2006

1. The Crisis of Democracy and the Public Library

Public libraries account for a miniscule portion of government expenditures and are the first to be cut when budgets fall short. Government policymakers view public libraries as a dispensable supplement to the public school system, an inessential social service for the unemployed, or even as frivolous entertainment at public expense. So why should we care if barbarians crash the gates of the public library? Of what great significance to the state and its public would that be?

The answer is that government policymakers have missed the most important function of a public library, which is to promote and sustain the knowledge and values necessary for a democratic civilization. Conversely, the condition of public libraries may be taken as a litmus test for the state of democratic civilization. Any threat to the core values of a democratic civilization will be reflected in the state of its public libraries; and, any threat to public libraries will weaken democracy.

The main body of this work is occupied with an analysis of postmodern consumer capitalism and its effects on democratic civilization. We will find that postmodern consumer capitalism threatens the public sphere of rational discourse and that the healthy functioning of this sphere is essential to democracy. Postmodern consumer capitalism transforms discourse into a private consumer product and as such reduces knowledge to mere information or entertainment. But since public libraries play such an important role in maintaining the public sphere of rational discourse I have framed my analysis of postmodern consumer capitalism with a discussion about the public library. The public library may be like the proverbial canary in the mine—the first to go when the air is poisoned. It is uniquely positioned to feel the effects of a declining democratic civilization; and it is the first to go when knowledge gets reduced to information and entertainment.

In March of 1998 the American Library Association (ALA) published an article by Steve Coffman in which he proposed that public libraries be run like corporate chain bookstores. The following issue of the ALA's magazine *American Libraries* hosted a large number of letters from librarians who objected to Coffman's proposal that libraries be run like bookstores. The author of one letter explained that a library is "a democratic, egalitarian center" that "provides a wide spectrum of information to anyone who wants it, regardless of their background." A bookstore, on the other hand, "has no mission, morality, vision, or even stake in the community; its only purpose is to get middle-class people to spend money."

Several years later Coffman's article looks more like a forecast or description of trends affecting public libraries than a radical proposal for change. Some libraries are already moving in the direction of imitating the organizational and procedural structure of corporate chain bookstores. The chain bookstores don't hire librarians. They hire low-paid clerks to help patrons fetch books. There is no reference service. Book ordering is centralized and automated. There is no discrimination between "good" literature and "bad" literature; there is no mission to serve the public good; there is no mission to promote democracy or education; the sole criterion for selecting books is sales/circulation. The most extreme example of this trend may be the branch libraries of east London which have been renamed "Idea Stores" (Lane, 2003; Ezard, 2003). The Idea Stores employ supervisors and customer service representatives, but no librarians. There are cafes near the entrance to each Idea Store but no reference service is available. Corporate designers and advertising agencies seek to draw "customers" into the Idea Stores by creating an appealing brand image. "The project—described as retail-inspired—is based on the conviction that 'in our increasingly retail-focused and lifestyle-conscious world' commerce is now the ruling influence on the lives of younger people. This group, it is felt, is far more likely to borrow books or use educational services if the ambience reminds them of a superstore or, as with the colours and signs at Bow, the departure lounge at Gatwick airport." (Ezard, 2003). In the United States, the public library system of Riverside County, serving a million people in California, was turned over to a private contractor in 1997 (Hanley, 1998: B6). The mayor of Jersey City's attempt to privatize his city's public library was beaten back by librarians and public spirited citizens in 1998, as was the Hawaii State Library's attempt to outsource book selection to Baker & Taylor in 1997 (Hanley, 1998). But GATS (General Agreement on Trade in Services) and the WTO could some day require all of the world's public libraries to privatize in the interest of neoliberal market reforms (Rikowski, 2003).

How did we get to the point of having libraries without librarians? How did we lose the 'public' in 'public library'? And why should we care? To answer these questions we will have to delve into the history of libraries and librarianship as well as explore larger trends in politics and the economy. We will need to think about the mission of a public library and what distinguishes it in a fundamental and essential way from a private market business. We will need to think about the difference between entertainment and education, pandering and edification, a market economy and democracy. What we will find is that democracy, civil education and the public good are the three pillars supporting the public library. Postmodern consumer capitalism threatens all three and with them the institution of the public library.

2. Democracy and the Profession of Librarianship

In a recently published history of libraries, Battles (2003) explains that prior to the nineteenth century libraries were by necessity limited to a small collection of classics because, in spite of the invention of the printing press, books remained difficult and expensive to produce. Book selection was therefore a simple process, since there was little to choose from, and it constituted a small part of librarianship. With the development of the mechanical mass production of books in the nineteenth century librarians were for the first time faced with the task of deciding which books from among the thousands produced they should add to their collections. Most of the first generation of public librarians were concerned about the flood of trashy popular literature made possible by mechanical mass production in the nineteenth century. They conceived their role to be "gatekeepers" of the culture and defenders of such public goods as democracy, education and morality. Some wanted to separate the wheat from the chaff and maintain a collection of great works. Others were willing to allow works of lesser value into their collections in the interest of providing their patrons with the first rung on a ladder of development that ascended toward the classics of western civilization. In either case, librarians maintained a collection of great works and understood their role to be that of educators who serve the public good.

Although Melvil Dewey accepted the same Victorian values as his colleagues, he did not believe that librarians should have the authority to instill those values in their patrons by directing their reading. Dewey's primary contribution to librarianship was to improve the efficiency of librar-

ies by adopting the techniques and strategies of mass production in factories. One such technique was standardization. Another was to dumb down skilled workers. Just as
scientific management in factories dumbed down skilled
craftsmen by putting all intelligent decision making into the
hands of managers and turning workers into virtual
automatons (such as Charlie Chaplin parodied in the classic film *Modern Times*), Dewey dumbed down professional
librarians.

Dewey was no pioneer in women's rights, in spite of
admitting women to the school of library science at Columbia. On the contrary, according to Battles (2003: 144),
Dewey used the hiring of women in libraries to define the
profession down. Since women in Victorian society were
generally subordinate to men and lacked professional
autonomy, by installing women in libraries Dewey hoped
not to raise the status of women but to lower the status of
librarians. By installing women in libraries Dewey wished
to insure that librarians would defer to male professionals
such as himself. For Dewey the role of librarians was akin
to that of factory workers. Their role was to execute a mechanical work process in the most efficient manner possible, as determined by their managers and other experts,
not to design or direct that process. The role of librarians
was to get books into the hands of their patrons as efficiently as possible by following Dewey's scientifically designed work procedures. As mere technical functionaries
Dewey did not believe that librarians should have the
authority to direct the reading of their patrons by selecting
books they deemed best.

The Carnegie Corporation, which funded so many of
America's first public libraries, had a similar view of the
role of librarians. Andrew Carnegie himself shared the prevailing moral views of his age. In his 1889 essay "Wealth"

Carnegie "stated why he believed he became rich: his mental and moral capabilities would enable him to use money to serve the public good." (Jones, 1997: 12). In a 1920 biography Carnegie was quoted as saying "I think I'm doing a whole lot for the morality of the country through my libraries." (Johnson, 1996: B8). But he repeatedly stated that his public library buildings weren't philanthropy because they "only help those who help themselves." (Jones, 1997: 11). On November 18, 1916 a Mr. Johnson submitted a report to the trustees of the Carnegie Corporation stating that "it was the librarian's training and aptitude that defined the impact of each library" and recommending, among other things, that the Carnegie Corporation should "spend money to support the academic training of librarians." (Jones, 1997: 101). But the trustees, led by Mr. Bertram, rejected Johnson's proposals. According to Johnson's autobiography, Bertram said that with regard to "librarian training, Mr. Carnegie . . . believed in having books where anyone could get ahold of them . . . a librarian's business is to hand out books, and that doesn't require a long expensive training." (quoted in Jones, 1997: 102).

However, in spite of these challenges to the professionalism of librarianship, librarians did receive academic training throughout the twentieth century, and for most of the twentieth century they conceived the primary mission of the public library to be the promotion of democracy through education. In her review of the history of the way in which librarians in the United States have understood their role in supporting democracy, Kathleen de la Pena McCook (2001) identifies four major publishing events: the histories of the public library by Jesse H. Shera and Sidney Ditzion, the reports of the American Library Association's Committee on Post-War Planning, and the set of volumes issued by the ALA's Public Library Inquiry. The histories

by Shera (1949) and Ditzion (1947) were the first major
histories of public library development. As McCook (2001)
emphasizes, both Shera and Ditzion recognized education
and democracy as central to the mission of the modern
public library throughout its history. According to Shera
(1949: vi): "The modern public library in large measure
represents the need of democracy for an enlightened elec-
torate, and its history records its adaptation to changing
social requirements." Ditzion (1947:74) states that during
the latter half of the nineteenth century public libraries in
the United States continued "the educational process
where the schools left off, and by conducting a people's
university, a wholesome capable citizenry would be fully
schooled in the conduct of a democratic life." The *National
Plan for Public Library Service* (1948) was the final part of the
work of the American Library Association's Committee on
Post-War Planning. The Public Library Inquiry was car-
ried out and published between 1947-1952. Both of these
reports of the American Library Association emphasized
that democracy and enlightened citizenship would be just
as important to the mission of the public library in the
years going forward as they had been in the century prior
to World War II.

Over the course of the 1960s and the 1970s, however,
the Public Library Association moved away from prescrib-
ing national standards toward introducing a planning
process by which each local library could develop its own
mission. As McCook (2001) explains: "Once the Public
Library Association developed the planning process, each
public library had a methodology to use at the local level to
develop its own mission, goals and objectives in collabora-
tion with community and staff. The 1980 manual, *Planning
for Results,* and the 1982 *Output Measures for Public Libraries*
provided the tools for planning and measurement. The role

of the public library in serving democracy was no longer a value imbedded in a formal public library standards document, for no such document existed at the national level." As we will see later, this shift from national standards to locally defined objectives corresponds to a shift in consumer capitalism from the homogeneous mass markets of the 1950s to the segmented markets and marketing strategies of the 1960s and the 1970s. Although the American Library Association continues to make statements in support of democracy up to the present day, and although the local determination of a library's mission could contribute to greater democracy rather than less, it should be noted that the quantitative nature of the *Output Measures for Public Libraries* (Zweizig, 1982) creates a bias toward measures of success in the public library which mirror measures of success in the capitalist economy. For example, circulation mirrors sales. Both circulation and sales can be easily measured in quantitative terms. But if democracy and an enlightened citizenry were the goals of the public library, then we would measure success not merely by how many items we circulate, but by how many readers we have helped to become better citizens. That in turn depends on the quality and diversity of material we circulate as well as their number and highlights the need for professional judgement in collection development. In fact, the decline of qualitative measures of success at the national level reflects the rise of consumer capitalism during the postwar years and the decline of the ideal of the democratic nation state. As we will see later this decline culminates in the 1990s with the rise of neoliberalism (Barber, 1995) and the notion of a market democracy (Frank, 2000) in which the consumer replaces the citizen as the primary agent of "democracy" or of what is being called democracy.

3. The Reasoning Public: Public Libraries, Democracy and the Public Good

The notion of the public good is essential to the notion of a public library. As early as the eighteenth century democracy was believed to be the public good and public education was thought necessary to fulfill that good. Thus modern public libraries were originally conceived as serving the public good by promoting democracy and civil education. But it was not always believed that democracy was a public good.

The notion of the public good precedes both liberalism and democracy. It arose with the development of the first modern states, which were absolute monarchies, not democracies. Feudal societies such as those which existed in Europe during the Middle Ages consist of a network of personal relationships. The primary relationship in a feudal society is the personal relationship of loyalty or fealty between lord and vassal. There is little or no conception of equality under a uniformly applied legal code serving an impersonal public good. There are only the private goods of lord and vassal. Early modern absolutist states in eighteenth century France and Prussia were the first to replace personal, feudal relationships with formal, legal structures of organization. Bolstering this trend was a revival of Roman law which replaced medieval laws of Germanic-feudal origin. As the size of the state bureaucracy surrounding the monarchy grew, its structure became more abstract and impersonal. A system of public law developed to regulate the state bureaucracy in the interest of a *salus publica* or common good. Although absolute monarchs created the first state bureaucracies, the organizational demands of these bureaucracies increasingly gave them a life of their own. State functionaries still owed loyalty to the monarch, but they did so not because they were obligated to serve the private interests of the monarch, but because the monarch was himself the first servant of the state and of the public good. In the "Prussian model" the "state was made transcendent over the physical person of its head through the depersonalization and objectification of its power. Public law shaped the state as an artificial, organizational entity operating through individuals who in principle were interchangeable and who in their official activities were expected to employ their certified abilities in stewardlike loyalty to the state and commitment to its interests." (Poggi, 1978: 76). The absolute monarch did, however, retain the right to define the public good and to set state policy accordingly. Generally the monarchs set state policy to reward social groups such as the rising bourgeoisie or older feudal estates who benefited the state in some way.

During the Enlightenment in the eighteenth century certain intellectual components of the bourgeoisie (in addition to smaller numbers of nobility and clergy) came to demand their right to develop and express a "public opinion" on matters of state and of the public good. According to Poggi (1978: 81) these components "had been developing a distinct social identity—that of a *public,* or rather, at first, of a variety of 'publics.' They had been increasingly carrying out their pursuits in distinctive settings and media (from scientific societies, literary salons, Masonic lodges, and coffeehouses to publishing houses and the daily periodical press) that were public in being accessible to all interested comers, or at least to all those possessing appropriate, objectively ascertainable qualifications, such as learning, technical competence, relevant information, persuasive eloquence, creative imagination, and capacity for critical judgment. Furthermore, all participants were allowed to contribute to the open-ended, relatively unconstrained process of argument intended to produce a widely held, critically established 'public opinion' about any given theme." These groups were, Poggi (1978: 82) tells us, seeking "to complement the 'public sphere' constructed from above with a 'public realm' formed by individual members of the civil society transcending their personal concerns, elaborating a 'public opinion' on matters of state and bringing it to bear on activities of state organs." This development led quite logically toward liberal democracy. "A 'reasoning public' might lead the civil society to break through the passive, subject position in which the official power sought to confine it. The reasoning public not only dared to open debate on matters that those powers had ever treated as *arcana imperii*, but threatened to extend that debate to wider and wider social circles in order to increase its support." (Poggi, 1978: 82)

Among the most important settings in which a "reasoning public" developed were the new subscription libraries of the eighteenth century. Prior to the introduction of these libraries only the very wealthy and the clergy had access to large numbers of books. The new subscription libraries of the eighteenth century provided a wider public with access to books. In 1731 Benjamin Franklin and members of the Junto, a philosophical association, established the Library Company. Beginning in the 1740s similar libraries were established in other American cities. Members of the Library Company chose as their motto the Latin phrase *Communiter Bona profundere Deum est* which translates as "to pour forth benefits for the common good is divine." (Ashby, 1977) On September 5, 1774 members of the First Continental Congress met at Carpenters' Hall in Philadelphia where the Library Company was housed and were given full use of the library. Nine signers of the Declaration of Independence were also members of the Library Company. And in 1787 the Library Company offered delegates to the Constitutional Convention use of its library. European liberals conceived of the mission of the library in similar terms. Antonio Panizzi was exiled from Modena, Italy because of "his attachment to secret societies that mixed liberal politics with quasi-Masonic mysticism." (Battles, 2003: 128) He fled to England where in 1837 he was appointed Keeper of the Printed Books at the British Museum, which held the largest collection of books in England. Panizzi's "work was informed all along by a democratic impulse, as he makes clear in this report. 'I want the poor student to have the same means of indulging his learned curiosity,' he wrote the trustees, 'of following his rational pursuits, of consulting the same authorities, of fathoming the most intricate inquiry as the richest man in the kingdom . . . and I contend that the government is bound to give him the most liberal and unlimited assistance in this respect'." (Battles, 2003: 131)

In 1838 the London radical William Lovett proposed a bill to Parliament he called the People's Charter and thereby inaugurated the Chartist movement which would represent the hopes of Britain's working class through the revolutionary year of 1848. The People's Charter included demands for universal male suffrage and the elimination of property qualifications for election to government office. The Chartists wished to expand the "reasoning public" to include the working class. The "Chartists recognized the importance of education in fulfilling the aspirations of those excluded from power and position. Throughout Britain in the mid-nineteenth century, Chartist reading rooms—cooperative lending libraries offering books to members of radical organizations—sprang up." (Battles, 2003: 135; similar reading rooms have emerged today in response to the inadequacy of state and capitalist library models, see Dodge, 1998)

John Stuart Mill, the utilitarian philosopher and the most important liberal intellectual of the Victorian era, agreed that wider access to education was necessary for the public good and that libraries were essential to providing such education. He differed from the Chartists, however, in his conception of the public good. For Mill capitalism could be reconciled with the moral values of liberal democracy and made to serve the public good. But for this to occur education and free access to information was necessary. "Mill said that the masses were 'bad calculators' who 'lacked practical good sense,' and that a sound education would turn them into good calculators: sober and sensible consumers, well-trained and aspiring workers. Among a class of intellectuals who had begun to believe that economic phenomena followed the universal laws revealed by reason, it made sense that by greater access to information, all people could be trained in reason's principles, turning themselves into rational actors for the greater good of all." (Battles, 2003: 136)

Thus in 1850 Parliament passed a public library bill. Soon public libraries supplanted subscription libraries and Chartist reading rooms. "When the Manchester Public Library opened in 1852, it occupied a former Chartist hall, and speakers at the opening ceremony couched their statements in the language of class war and reconciliation. . . . No less a light than Charles Dickens . . . was confident that libraries would teach 'that capital and labour are not opposed, but mutually dependant and mutually supporting'." (Battles, 2003: 137)

Although the early public libraries were intended to serve capitalism, it is important to note that nineteenth century liberals such as Mill believed that capitalism both presupposed certain moral values and produced a public good which transcended private economic interests. Educational institutions such as libraries were expected to instill these moral values in the public and thereby promote liberal capitalist democracy. As we will see later, capitalism in the twentieth century lost its moral underpinnings and purpose, while educational institutions lost their mission to edify the public. In postwar America, the public no longer reasoned or concerned itself with the common good, but was reduced to an aggregate of individual consumers seeking entertainment.

4. Education, Democracy and the Public Good

To understand why education was believed to be necessary for the public good, we must go back to the mechanical worldview that emerged during the scientific revolution of the seventeenth century and to its impact on theories of human nature. The scientific revolution of the seventeenth century was primarily a revolution in mathematical physics. It began with Galileo's discovery that terrestrial bodies fall to the earth according to a mathematical formula and with Kepler's discovery that planetary bodies move across the sky according to another mathematical formula. One of Descartes' greatest contributions to the new science was analytic geometry, the discovery that space could be understood algebraically. Descartes' analytic geometry reconciled geometry with algebra, space with number. Combined with the hypothesis that matter extended in space is the fundamental reality in the world, analytic geometry held out the promise for a mathematical account of the entire universe.

The scientific revolution culminated with Newton's discovery of the mathematical laws of mechanical motion. Newton's discovery that the same mathematical laws explained the motion of both terrestrial and celestial bodies suggested that the same mathematical laws applied to all material bodies everywhere. For example, the same mathematical laws could be used to explain both the fall of an apple from a tree and the elliptical orbits of the planets around the sun. Newton's invention of calculus built upon Descartes' analytic geometry to provide a powerful tool for the mathematical analysis of the mechanical motion of matter extended in space.

The success of the new mechanical physics in explaining the motion of inanimate bodies inspired many philosophers to wonder whether human experience and behavior could be explained in a similar way. In the seventeenth century Thomas Hobbes was the first philosopher to propose a theory of the human mind according to which the mind is composed of units of sensation received through the sense organs. These units of sensation may be combined or arranged in any variety of ways in order to create more complex ideas just as bits of matter extended in space may be combined or rearranged to create more complex structures. But all ideas or mental phenomena may ultimately be reduced to units of sensation. Later in the seventeenth century John Locke offered a more detailed account of this mechanical theory of the mind while (not altogether consistently) managing to preserve some of the moral principles of Christianity and the bourgeois class from which he derived. Locke's philosophy of mind in turn provided the philosophical foundation for the Enlightenment of the eighteenth century and the American revolution.

John Locke famously declared that at birth the mind is a *tabula rasa* or blank slate endowed only with the capacity for reflection but with nothing yet to reflect upon. The mind is completely empty until over the course of one's life it receives sensations through the sense organs. The mind has the power to combine or rearrange these sense impressions through its capacity for reflection, but it cannot create any new content. The difference between two minds is due entirely to different experiences, not to any innate difference between those minds.

Locke's mechanical-empirical theory of mind thus provided a radical alternative to the theory of human nature that held sway throughout the ancient and medieval worlds in which innate differences at birth were assumed to be the basis for a natural social hierarchy and division of labor. According to Plato, for example, there are three parts of the soul: the reasoning part, the spirited part, and the appetites. From birth different parts of the soul predominate in different individuals. Those born with an unusually great capacity to reason are suited to become leaders and statesmen. Those whose appetites are stronger than their capacity to reason are suited to become farmers and craftsmen. And those who are ruled by the spirited part of their soul are destined to become soldiers and warriors. Aristotle's conception of human nature was organic. Living beings are born with an innate potential to realize a particular form. For example, an acorn has an innate capacity to become an oak tree. The proper soil and climate may be necessary for the acorn to become an oak tree, but no amount of sunlight or fertilizer will allow the acorn to become a giraffe. Such a view of human nature suited the feudal world well, because under feudalism one's place in society was largely fixed at birth.

Under Locke's theory we are all born equal. Differences are due only to experience. By altering experience we alter whom we become. By altering whom we become we alter society. Education is a way of shaping experience to control whom we become. Thus education held the key to creating a better society.

The philosophers of the Enlightenment were not, however, naive about the challenges they faced. They did not believe the masses were ready yet for democracy, reserving that for the educated bourgeois such as themselves. Voltaire's position, says Randall, was typical:

> Divide the human race into twenty parts, and there
> will be nineteen composed of those who work with
> their hands, and who will never know that there

was a Locke in the world; in the twentieth part remaining, how few men are there who can read?
and among those who can, there will be twenty
who read romances, to one who studies science.
The number who can think is excessively small.
(Voltaire, quoted in Randall, 1940: 337)

Hence they were willing to work with absolute monarchs,
so long as those monarchs ruled by law and for the public
good, rather than by arbitrary fiat. Democracy for all remained the ideal, but in the meantime they were willing to
appeal to the power of the monarch to achieve that end.

According to Randall it was Helvetius who most explicitly drew out the democratic implications of Locke's
new theory of human nature. "Helvetius was one of the
group gathered about Diderot who hoped that a wise king,
by instituting the proper reforms in his dominions, especially in education, could bring about a millennium of sa-
gacious and noble citizens." (Randall, 1940: 316) Through
legislative reform the wise statesmen could make virtuous
men and good citizens. The king would therefore effectively become a moral educator.

The supreme ethical principle according to Helvetius
was "public utility" or *interet general* or *bonheur general.* The
supreme ethical principle was to act in such a way as to
yield the maximum pleasure compatible with a minimum
of pain in the whole of society. Jeremy Bentham, the English founder of utilitarianism, was a follower of Helvetius.
Like Helvetius, Bentham sought to place law on a more
rational foundation that would serve the public good. John
Stuart Mill in turn modified the principle of utility for the
Victorian era, belittling the value of sexual pleasure, for
example, whereas Bentham had not distinguished between
"higher" and "lower" pleasures and Helvetius had wanted

the state to reward its best citizens with the greatest sexual pleasures.

Helvetius' "faith in education led him to maintain the equality and similarity of all men at birth, and to disregard entirely any hereditary causes of individual differences." (Randall, 1940: 317) In opposition to those who assert that there are innate differences between minds Helvetius declared: "Qunitillian, Locke and myself, say, The inequality of minds is the effect of a known cause, and this cause is the difference of education." (quoted in Randall, 1940: 317) Thus the king's educational reforms would culminate in a democratic society of equal citizens. It was with such reforms in mind that Helvetius dedicated his second work to Catherine II of Russia, "who toyed with such ideas and called Diderot to St. Petersburg to institute the new order." (Randall, 1940: 318)

There was a conservative streak running through the age of the Enlightenment which sought to protect the propertied middle class from the "mob." In the United States John Adams, leader of the Federalist Party, sought to protect private property from both the power of monarchs and the people. "We may appeal to every page of history we have hitherto turned over, for proofs irrefragable, that the people, when they have been unchecked, have been just as unjust, tyrannical, brutal, barbarous and cruel as any king or senate possessed of uncontrollable power." (John Adams, quoted in Randall, 1940: 348) Not such a mob should rule, Adams believed, but rather the "natural aristocracy of the wise, the rich and the good" set off from the mass of "simple men, the laborers, husbandmen, mechanics, and merchants in general, who pursue their occupations and industry without any knowledge in liberal arts or sciences, or in anything but their own trades or pursuits." (John Adams, quoted in Randall, 1940: 349)

When Enlightenment thinkers granted the franchise to a broader public than landowners, they did so on the condition that the public be educated in the way that the best of the English gentry may have been. This was true even of the most radical democratic theories of the Enlightenment, including Rousseau's, which was popularized in the United States during the nineteenth century by the party of Jefferson and Jackson.

According to Rousseau, the state ought to serve the interests of the people. But the state should not necessarily obey the actual vote of the majority, because the majority may vote against its own best interest. According to Rousseau a legitimate state must rest on the principle of the social contract. The authority of the state does not derive from God or from the King's ancestors but from the consent of the governed. However, Rousseau distinguished between the "will of all" and the "general will." The "will of all" is simply what the people actually desire, for example, how they actually vote. The "general will," on the other hand, is what the people would want if the people were sufficiently well informed to know what their best interests were. A legitimate state requires the consent of both the "will of all" and the "general will." But since the "will of all" and the "general will" do not necessarily coincide some mechanism must be put in place to insure that they do. That mechanism is public education. Education of the public is necessary to insure that the majority vote coincides with the best interest of the people.

> When will men actually know what is best for
> them? Obviously only when they are educated and
> wise. Hence it is no accident that from Rousseau
> down all democratic theorizers have insisted on the
> cardinal importance of education. Without an in-

telligent citizenry, majority rule, and with it all
hope of combining liberty with law, becomes quite
impossible. (Randall, 1940: 353)

Indeed as far along as 1946 Wilhelm Reich would write in
The Mass Psychology of Fascism about the obligation of the
state to educate the masses. It is better, Reich says, if the
change from state administration of the people to self administration by the people occurs organically and without
bloodshed.

But this is possible only if the representatives of the
state above society are fully conscious of the fact
that they are nothing but the delegated executive
organs of the working human community; that, in
the strictest sense of the word, they are executive
organs from necessity, i.e., they are executive organs made necessary by the ignorance and wretch-
edness in which millions of people live. Strictly
speaking, they have the tasks of good educators,
namely the task of making self-reliant adults of the
children entrusted to their care. A society that is
striving to attain genuine democracy must never
lose sight of the principle that it is the task of the
state to make itself more and more superfluous, just
as an educator becomes superfluous when he has
done his duty toward the child. If this principle is
not forgotten, bloodshed can be and will be
avoided. Only to the extent to which the state
clearly and unequivocally abolishes itself is it possible for work-democracy to develop *organically;* conversely, to the same extent to which the state tries
to externalize itself and to forget its educational
task, it provokes human society to remind it that it
came into being from necessity and must also dis-
appear from necessity. (Reich, 1970: 283)

The state which does not educate the people for self-rule is, Reich warns us, a fascist state.

In *Democracy's Discontents* (1996) the political philosopher Michael Sandel explains that republican theory has always required citizens to be actively engaged in rational deliberation with their fellow citizens about the nature of the common good and that this in turn requires that citizens receive an education in public affairs and civic virtue. According to republican political theory, self-rule "means deliberating with fellow citizens about the common good and helping to shape the destiny of the political community. But to deliberate well about the common good requires more than the capacity to choose one's ends and to respect others' rights to do the same. It requires a knowledge of public affairs and also a sense of belonging, a concern for the whole, a moral bond with the community whose fate is at stake. To share in self-rule therefore requires that citizens possess, or come to acquire, certain qualities of character, or civic virtues." (Sandel, 1996: 5-6) The republican conception of liberty requires a formative politics that "cultivates in citizens the qualities of character self-government requires." What Sandel calls the "liberal" conception of liberty, on the other hand, conceives persons as "free and independent selves, unencumbered by moral or civic ties they have not chosen." According to Sandel the republican theory predominated earlier in American history but has declined in recent decades. Later we will see how the decline of the republican conception of liberty is related to the rise of consumer capitalism.

The state's need and obligation to educate the people in order to sustain a democratic society has been enshrined in the laws of the United States. In 2001 Justice Leland DeGrasse of the State Supreme Court in Manhattan ruled that New York State's formula for public school financing was unconstitutional because it deprived students in New York City of their constitutional right to a sound, basic education. But what constitutes a "sound, basic education"? In his ruling Justice DeGrasse appealed to the example of jury service as a litmus test for a sound, basic education. A citizen has received a sound, basic education if he or she has acquired sufficient cognitive skill to function effectively on a jury (Archibold, 2001). Together with participation in elections, jury service is a key component of democracy in the United States. Thus a "sound, basic education" is one which allows the people to function effectively as citizens of a democratic society.

5. Education, Edification, Entertainment and Consumption

Soon after I had begun working for a large, urban public library in 1992 I was invited to talk with an elderly administrator who was about to retire after a long career which she began as a children's librarian. She was aware of my previous teaching experience and in the privacy of her office she explained to me that education was not the mission of the library. "I consider myself an entertainer," she said, "not an educator." But in fact she taught me a great deal, because she instigated a process of reflection lasting many years in which I have tried to understand the meaning of her words. What is the difference between education and entertainment? Did entertainment replace education as the mission of the library and if so, why? In this section I will focus primarily on the first question.

Education is the consumption of information for the purpose of improving our understanding and, insofar as desire depends upon understanding, of improving our moral and aesthetic choices. Thus education is edifying as well as illuminating. Entertainment on the other hand is the consumption of information for the purpose of pleasure only. It is neither educational nor edifying. Education and edification do not necessarily exclude pleasure. Pleasure is necessarily a part of education insofar as education makes higher levels of pleasure and the pleasurable consumption of information possible. We consume education and we are pleasured by it. But it is possible to consume information without being educated or edified.

A great deal of popular literature falls into the category of information that is neither educational nor edifying. At best it is entertaining. How-to and self-help books provide simplistic instructions on how to achieve what we desire. They do not challenge us to question our desires or our beliefs about them. Wendy Kaminer, who has written a series of excellent books critical of the self-help industry in the United States, complained about the adverse effect of self-help books on education and democracy in *I'm Dysfunctional, You're Dysfunctional:*

> Some will call me an elitist for disdaining popular self-help literature and the popular recovery movement; but a concern for literacy and critical thinking is only democratic. The popularity of books comprising slogans, sound bites, and recipes for success is part of a larger, frequently bemoaned trend blamed on television and the failure of public education and blamed for political apathy. . . . recently the fascination with self-help has made a significant contribution to the dumbing down of general interest books and begun changing the relationship between writers and readers; it is less collegial and collaborative than didactic. Today, even critical books about ideas are expected to be prescriptive, to conclude with simple, step-by-step solutions to whatever crisis they discuss. Reading itself is becoming a way out of thinking. (quoted in Washburn and Thornton, 1996: 33-34)

Reading as entertainment is a passive act of consumption. Reading as education is part of a process of inquiry. The reader brings questions to the text but is transformed in the process of reading to ask new questions which lead to yet other texts. Reading as education is work in the sense that it requires active engagement on the part of the reader.

The notion that high culture is hard brain-work is, says William A. Henry III, true. But,

> American popular culture does not embrace this certification of art as work. Indeed the word *art* is rarely used at all. The preferred signifier is the word *entertainment*, which correctly conveys that the aspirations are generally escapist, nostalgic, or anodyne. Entertainment promises to make you feel better, to help you forget your troubles, to liberate you from having to think. Even when entertainment touches deep feelings, it does so as a gesture of reassurance, a combination of sentiment and sloganeering. This is what most people say they want, and the market lets them have it without anyone in a position of intellectual or social leadership telling them that they should ask more of themselves—and might benefit thereby. (quoted in Washburn and Thornton, 1996: 30-31)

Thus readers of popular imaginative literature do not seek to enrich their understanding or to be edified or even to enhance their capacity for enjoyment. They seek only to vicariously enjoy the thrills, sensations and pleasures of imagined characters and events. Consequently, popular imaginative literature is generally formulaic, with each book essentially the same as the one before it, repeating the same themes, characters and plot structures over and over again.

The distinction between education and entertainment, edifying one's audience or pandering to them, is central to Plato's philosophy and reverberates throughout Western history. For Plato, the distinction between education and entertainment reflects a long series of other binary oppositions including being and becoming, truth and illusion, the intellect and the senses, the soul and the body. But even a materialist and an empiricist like Helvetius, who would not accept all of these other oppositions, agreed with most of Plato's ideas on education and the state. Like Plato, Helvetius believed that the true statesman is an educator and that the state has an obligation to educate the public. For Plato, not everyone is predisposed to receive the same level of education. For Helvetius, we are all born with an equal capacity for education. But both would agree that the state ought to educate the public and that pandering is a mark of corruption. Both would take an admission from a public library administrator that she is an entertainer but not an educator as a sign of a debased civilization.

Plato's philosophy is an intricate web of recursive analogues. An analogue has the form "a is to b as c is to d," or using symbolic notation, a:b::c:d, or again, using mathematical notation, $a/b = c/d$. The musical scale has the form of an analogue because the relationship between notes within each octave is the same. Notes can be assigned numbers equal to the length of a monochord that would produce them, so the relationship between notes can be represented by a numerical proportion. For Plato, like his predecessor Pythagoras, music, mathematics, and philosophy are analogues of one another because the relationship between their parts is the same.

In the *Republic* Plato describes the ideal state and the course of education that would be necessary to sustain it. Plato believes that the true statesman, the philosopher-king, is an educator. In the examples below taken from the *Gorgias* Plato sheds light on the relationship between education and entertainment by drawing analogies to various professions or arts.

Plato distinguished between arts that pander to the body's immediate desires and professions that aim to satisfy only those desires that are good. Educators and statesmen belong to the second category. An example Plato used to shed light on this distinction is the difference between a confectioner or baker of cakes and a doctor of medicine. Plato wants to suggest that the difference between a doctor and a confectioner is analogous to the difference between a philosopher-king and a doctor. The doctor does what is really good for the patient's body instead of what merely appears to be good. The philosopher-king does what is really good for the citizens by improving their souls instead of what merely appears to be good by only treating their bodies.

The confectioner does not distinguish between good and bad pleasures. Any cake that tastes good and gives the customer pleasure is a good cake. The only way a confectioner has of telling whether a cake is good or not is to taste it. If the cake produces a pleasurable sensation then it's a good cake. A cake that was not pleasurable or was even painful would be a bad cake. The doctor on the other hand distinguishes between good and bad pleasures and pains. A medical treatment may be painful but still be very good for the patient. Eating too much cake may be very pleasurable but is not good for the patient. Bitter medicine may be better than tasty cake. The doctor uses his or her reasoning skills and medical education rather than the patient's immediate sensations alone to distinguish between good and bad medical treatments. Thus the doctor is methodical and can give a rational account of his or her actions. Confectionery cannot give a rational account of its actions because it relies solely upon sensation rather than reason to distinguish between good and bad. Confectionery is an example of what Plato calls a "knack." A "knack" is an ability to do something without being able to give a rational account of one's actions. Medicine is an example of a profession because its practitioners can give a rational account of their actions. In general a profession is an occupation in which its practitioners can give a rational account in speech or writing of how their practices serve the good of their clients. In giving a rational account the professional educates others into the profession. A knack on the other hand cannot be taught because there is no rational account to give the student. A knack is learned through imitation and through trial and error.

In another analogy Plato compares a beautician to a physical trainer. The beautician, he says, produces merely a fleeting appearance of health and strength, whereas the physical trainer produces a more enduring reality. Similarly, entertainers produce words and images which give us immediate pleasure but have no lasting beneficial effect, whereas educators produce words and images which may not be immediately pleasant to receive but which edify or serve the real good of their audience. In general when professionals produce or provide words and images for an audience they must do so in such a way that they edify rather than pander to their audience. To do that they must themselves possess a rational understanding of the good. And to do that they must have undergone a rigorous course of philosophical education, since philosophy is rational knowledge of the good.

In Plato's dialogues the figure of Socrates exemplifies the virtues of a responsible professional. Socrates is brought to trial by corrupt politicians on charges of corrupting the youth of Athens. Corrupt politicians "gratify their hearers, sacrificing the public interest to their own personal success, and treating their audience like children, whom their only object is to please . . . but true virtue consists in fulfilling those desires whose satisfaction makes a man better and denying those which make him worse." (Plato, 1960: 110)

Socrates will not pander to the crowd even to save his own life. "Am I to withstand the Athenians with the idea of improving them, like a doctor, or to behave like a servant whose object is simply to do his master's pleasure?" (Plato, 1960: 138-139) Socrates knows that he cannot win against those who pander to the crowd, but he courageously asserts that it is better to suffer harm than do wrong.

> So because what I say on any occasion is not designed to please, and because I aim not at what is most agreeable but at what is best, and will not employ the subtle arts which you advise, I shall have no defence to offer in a court of law. I can only repeat what I was saying to Polus; I shall be like a doctor brought before a tribunal of children at the suit of a confectioner. Imagine what sort of defence a man like that could make before such a court if he were accused in the following terms: 'Children, the accused has committed a number of crimes against you; he is the ruin of even the youngest among you with his surgery and cautery; he reduces you to a state of helpless misery by choking you with bitter draughts and inflicting upon you a regime of starvation which cuts you off from food and drink. What a contrast to the abundant and varied luxury with which I have entertained you.' What do you think that the doctor could find to say in such a plight? If he were to utter the truth and tell the children that he had done all these things in the interest of their health, think of the prodigious outcry that a court so constituted would raise. (Plato, 1960: 140)

Education presupposes professional authority based on knowledge. The purpose of education is to edify students. The purpose of entertainment is to give the customers what they want. It presupposes no distinction between right and wrong because the customer is always right. Entertainment is a species of consumerism. In a postmodern information economy such as the United States entertainment is big

business. Education is not a business at all but a public
service whose aim is to improve society, not merely in appearance, but in reality.

6. From Ethical Liberalism to Economic Liberalism

As we have seen, even before the development of liberalism and democracy, the modern world replaced the private power of feudal lords with the public realm of the state. The state served the public good as defined by the monarch. Private property remained, but it did not automatically confer on its owners any special legal or political privileges. Political and legal power was centralized and concentrated in the hands of the monarch. Neither free elections nor free markets were originally believed to be necessary for the public good. Mercantilism was the reigning economic doctrine of the day, and it allowed monarchs to interfere in foreign trade to protect the national interest. The American revolution was in large measure a rebellion against mercantilism and a triumph for classic liberal economic doctrine.

According to liberal economic doctrine, property owners should compete with one another on a level playing field. Market players must follow the same rules or laws designed to serve the common good. But in practice, the power that private property confers upon its owners has always threatened to overwhelm the public good. The classic liberal economists attempted to resolve this apparent contradiction between the public good and private property by showing how the free market serves a moral purpose. In a somewhat circular manner, however, they recognized that the market would serve a moral purpose only if certain conditions, including the moral development of individuals, were present.

The moral values which the Victorian liberals believed the market both served to produce and presupposed were the values of Puritanism. Today we are inclined to think of the market as a means for consumption or the satisfaction of one's desires. But the Victorian liberals believed that the market entailed an almost ascetic restraint of the body and its wants. Indeed, the Victorian liberals believed that the market served to cultivate an entire array of middle class values, all of which can be understood as variations on the theme of the moral restraint of the body and its desires. These values "included, to cite some of those gathered together by the high priest of Victorian 'character' building—Samuel Smiles (1812-1905)—self-culture, self-control, energy, industry, frugality, thrift, prudence, patience, perseverance, honesty, integrity, temperance, sobriety, independence, manliness and duty." (Bellamy, 1992: 10)

According to the classic liberal economist David Ricardo, capital served as the mainspring of the economy. By investing his wealth in the means of production rather than spending it on consumption the capitalist served to increase the economy's productive capacity. But the act of reinvesting one's wealth in the means of production rather than spending it on consumption presupposes the moral values of self-restraint trumpeted by Samuel Smiles. For only by denying one's bodily instincts and desires by sheer force of character can one abstain from consumption. Thus Ricardo and other classic liberal economists believed that economic growth and prosperity depended upon moral restraint.

During the Victorian era John Stuart Mill was the chief spokesperson for the view that the market could be reconciled with morality and the public good. Mill argued that a liberal market would produce the greatest good for the greatest number and would therefore serve the public good. Mill's moral theory was a version of utilitarianism adapted to the values of Victorian Puritanism and the needs of the burgeoning commercial market. Mill agreed with Jeremy Bentham that individuals are motivated by the pursuit of pleasure and that the public good could be defined as the greatest pleasure for the greatest number, but unlike Bentham he believed that the moral and intellectual pleasures were greater than the pleasures of the body. This key change to Bentham's psychology allowed Mill to argue that a free society had a better chance for moral development than one that was socially engineered from above.

For Mill the purpose of individual liberty and free markets is to promote the development of moral character which in turn would promote the public good. Mill believed that given the freedom to choose individuals would pursue their own moral development since the moral pleasures are greater than the pleasures of the body. "Mill's theory traded on an implicitly teleological and optimistic view of human nature, in which free agents naturally opted for 'higher' pleasures over the 'lower', 'Socratic dissatisfaction' over 'swinish contentment'. Moreover, Mill assumed that this refinement of human pleasures brought with it 'the better development of [the individual's] nature' and especially 'the feelings and capacities which have the good of others for their object'." (Bellamy, 1992: 24)

Liberty was not, therefore, an absolute value. Liberty was a means to an end. Under certain conditions liberty served to promote individual character and to produce the greatest good for the greatest number. If those conditions were not present, however, coercive measures could be taken to obtain them. These conclusions derived not only from Mill's utilitarianism, but also from the empiricist psychology he shared with most other members of the British philosophical tradition. "Mill's empiricist psychology

committed him to the thesis that we were largely formed by
our environment and history. The capacity for autonomy,
therefore, was a product of antecedent circumstances." As
a result, "Mill could justify considerable intervention and
provision on the part of the state or well-placed individuals
in order to give people the capacity for autonomy . . ."
(Bellamy, 1992: 25) Persons lacking in moral character or
the capacity for autonomy might not be given the same
freedoms as those who possessed them. Mill "explicitly excluded from his doctrine the non-autonomous, such as children and 'those backward states of society in which the
race itself may be considered in its nonage'. Indeed, he asserted 'despotism is a legitimate mode of government with
barbarians, provided the end be their improvement, and
the means justified by actually effecting that end.' Paternal-
istic interference with those who had yet to become
autonomous was both acceptable and imperative for Mill,
so long as the attainment of autonomy was the purpose and
effect of the measures." (Bellamy, 1992: 25-26)

In cases such as these Mill invokes the power of the enlightened statesman to educate the people for freedom. In
the opening chapters of his *Considerations of Representative Government* Mill declared that government served two purposes:
it operated "as an agency of national education" and it
supplied "arrangements for conducting the collective affairs
of the community in the state of education in which they
already are." (quoted in Bellamy, 1992: 27) Besides children and barbarians, the working class too required moral
education. "In liberal eyes the political ascendancy of the
masses had to be linked to their moral improvement if a
destructive anarchy was not to result. This was achieved in
two ways: first, by apparently extending the rewards and
values of the Victorian ethos to ever larger sections of the
community, and second by reinforcing the practice of its

distinctive virtues through a vast network of institutions—
from elementary schools and Mechanics Institutes to
friendly societies, co-operatives and savings banks." (Bellamy, 1992: 12-13) Public libraries would of course come to
be included in this vast network of institutions serving to
edify the masses. For the Victorians that meant instilling
the individualistic values of self-reliance espoused by Samuel Smiles. As Andrew Carnegie would proudly declare, his
public libraries "only helped those who helped themselves."

But Andrew Carnegie and the other Robber Barons
contributed to the decline of Victorian liberalism. The classic liberals believed that an invisible hand would move society towards material and moral improvement. But from
about 1870 on Western societies developed further and
further away from the ideal of a perfectly competitive market of small entrepreneurs which the theory of ethical liberalism presupposed. Liberals acknowledged that state intervention in the economy was necessary to prevent devia-
tions from the ideal market and to remedy the market's
"deficiencies in providing certain public goods. However,
they hoped the evolution of human sentiments would ultimately overcome these anti-social tendencies. When this
moral improvement failed to materialize, the state took on
a commensurately greater role as the ethical educator of a
recalcitrant populace." (Bellamy, 1992: 4) When these efforts failed, "the state itself became an instrument of the
very economic interests it sought to curb." Thus in the absence of a moral consensus ethical liberalism gave way in
the twentieth century to "economic liberalism," to a form
of liberalism no longer tempered by moral restraints or the
imperative to serve the public good, but in which the market becomes its own measure of what is good. Poggi (1978:
134) draws a similar conclusion, writing that the legitimacy

of the post-liberal state occurs "through acts of rule that assist the economic system in producing an ever-increasing flow of goods and services for the consumer." The relation between the public and private realm is reversed and obliterated, as the public realm of the state is made to serve the private economic interests of the market.

7. Coney Island and the Rise of Mass Entertainment

In the United States mass consumer markets first appeared with the industrial expansion following the Civil War and the construction of a national train system. Traveling on those trains along with raw materials and manufactured products was a new form of entertainment known as the circus. Whereas the carnivals of pre-industrial agrarian society were rituals enacted by the people in which the normal social hierarchy was temporarily inverted, the circus was a spectacle of freaks and curiosities to be observed by those who remained within the normal bounds of the social order. The Coney Island amusement park at the turn of the century took up where the circus left off and in turn anticipated vaudeville, the nickelodeon and the cinema. Coney Island was one of the first and best examples of entertainment for the urban industrial masses and as such provides us with an especially good opportunity to observe the clash between the values of Victorian liberalism and those of twentieth century consumerism.

According to Plato the structure of the soul is analogous to the structure of society. Both contain three parts. In the soul there are the appetites, the spirited part, and reason. In society there are the farmers and craftsmen, the warriors, and the philosophers. Just as reason ought to control the appetites in the soul, the philosopher-kings ought to rule the farmers and craftsmen. Inversion of this hierarchy causes tyranny in society and madness in the soul.

To contemporary critics Coney Island was a carnival that threatened to invert the social and psychic order by releasing the human animal from moral and rational con-

trol. "After the species of straightjacket that we wear in
every-day life is removed at such Saturnalia as Coney Island," James Gibbons Huneker observed in the 1910s, "the
human animal emerges in a not precisely winning guise."
(quoted in Kasson, 1978: 96) The human animal, or in
Freudian terms, the "id," craves release from reason and
reality. "Unreality is as greedily craved by the mob as alco-
hol by the dipsomaniac; indeed, the jumbled nightmares of
a morphine eater are actually realized at Luna Park." The
fact that so many people who visited Coney Island were
immigrants from Southern and Eastern Europe who did
not share Huneker's Puritan heritage added to Huneker's
fears of lunacy at Coney Island because according to the
dominant school of American psychiatry at the turn of the
century, the Puritan values of self-restraint typified by
Samuel Smiles "safeguarded not only family and society
but sanity itself." But the dangers were there for anyone
who entered Coney Island because "by encouraging sensu-
ous self-abandon," Coney Island "in a very real sense pro-
moted lunacy." (Kasson, 1978: 97)

The "id" is a pool of biological drives or appetites craving release from the constraints imposed upon it by the
"ego" and the "superego." The "ego" imposes reality testing on all of our thoughts, separating objective reality from
subjective fantasy. The "superego" imposes moral constraints, separating socially possible behavior from subjective desire. Freud claimed in *Civilization and Its Discontents*
that liberation of the id could only mean the collapse of
civilization. And beginning in the 1890s social psycholo-
gists in Europe and the United States argued that people
lost their usual psychological restraints when they gathered
together with others in large numbers. Thus the "mob psychology" of crowds and mass culture threatened to undermine civilization and introduce a new barbarism. "Once

en masse," Huneker warned darkly, "humanity sheds its civilization and becomes half child, half savage. . . . It will lynch an innocent man or glorify a scamp politician with equal facility. Hence the monstrous debauch of the fancy at Coney Island, where New York chases its chimera of pleasure." (Huneker, quoted in Kasson, 1978: 96) Huneker's worst fears of mass culture may have been realized in the twentieth century, but not exactly in the way he anticipated. Entertainment does pander to our desires rather than educate or edify. But it does so in order to make money. Entertainment is not carnival. It does not induce states of ecstasy or madness or liberate the id. It does not invert the social order or threaten authority. Entertainment is a commodified spectacle. Entertainment is the flip side of a capitalist economy that continues to require discipline and authority.

> Coney Island was necessarily an imperfect Feast of Fools, an institutionalized bacchanal. It represented a festival that did not express joy *about* something, but offered 'fun' in a managed celebration for commercial ends. Dispensing standardized amusement, it demanded standardized responses. Beneath the air of liberation, its pressures were profoundly conformist, its means fundamentally manipulative. . . . Coney Island's managers aimed always to . . . engineer the environment so as to keep customers in the role of consumers. Amusement parks thus pioneered merchandising techniques that designers of shopping malls would later adopt . . . (Kasson, 1978: 105-106)

Of course, in representing carnival, popular culture always runs the risk of fomenting actual carnival. But when this happens as it did in the late 1960s the old arguments from the Victorian era are dusted off and used again to put the carnival back into its commodified bottle. The fashions are patented and sold while the experience is prohibited, simply because the fashions are more profitable. What changed in the mass culture of the twentieth century was not the presence of repressive authority but the way in which authority was legitimated. In the twentieth century ethical liberalism was replaced by what Bellamy calls economic liberalism. Whereas previously, authority was legitimated by reference to a moral truth grounded in theology or the belief in God, in the twentieth century, capitalism became autonomous, justifying itself in its own terms without reference to any moral truth outside of itself. To nineteenth century liberals the ultimate purpose of economic activity was not profit but moral improvement. Indeed, according to classic liberal economic theory, the ideal market yields little or no profit. In a perfectly competitive market of small entrepreneurs, profit lures new producers into the market. As supplies increase, prices and profits fall, until a new equilibrium is reached where profits are too low to lure new producers into the market. Large and sustainable profits are possible only when competitors are restricted from entering the market. In other words, profits are possible only when the market is not free or liberal. Therefore ethical liberals asserted that the purpose of the market was not profit but moral improvement. In the twentieth century, however, liberals lost their faith that the market could serve a moral purpose. The purpose of economic exchange became simply more economic exchange. As the formula for capital would have it:

$$m \longrightarrow C \longrightarrow m + \Delta m$$

Money, which has no other use than as a medium of exchange for other economic goods, when exchanged for capital, creates more money, with greater exchange value, which can in turn be invested to create yet greater exchange value.

To those who wish to preserve the values of the Enlightenment, such as the philosopher Jurgen Habermas, this turn of events represents a crisis in legitimation. But to the postmodernists, paradoxical self-referential systems are simply the way "texts" work. Later we will examine in greater detail the postmodern logic of the "infotainment" economy. But for now we return to the ethical liberals and their objections to Coney Island.

Liberals at the turn of the century objected to Coney Island and other forms of mass entertainment because they were created for financial gain and promised the audience only pleasure. To rescue society from the dangers of profit and pleasure, greed and lust, reformers "advocated a characteristic progressive solution: government regulation and expert supervision. Under enlightened municipal auspices, recreation could serve as a powerfully constructive force in social integration and moral development." (Kasson, 1978: 101-102) Thus public parks, gymnasiums, community centers and libraries would serve to instill a sense of "common purpose and democratic faith" and "habits of discipline and cooperation." The progressive reformers shared with the empiricist philosophers of the Enlightenment the faith that humans are a product of their environment and that education could therefore shape human behavior toward desirable ends. To the progressives "society as a whole was an educational institution and one which cried out for curricular reform." (Kasson, 1978: 104)

What the ethical liberals objected to at Coney Island, then, was that its purpose was only profit for its owners and pleasure for its patrons. To visit Coney Island was to consume an experience. It was to be entertained. Coney Island served to neither educate nor edify. It improved no one. It served no public good. It produced merely momentary pleasure. While many of its critics feared that in its abandonment to pleasure and sensation Coney Island resembled the ecstatic release of carnival, in hindsight it is clear that Coney Island represented a powerful shift from an early industrial economy which depended upon the ascetic moral habits of productive work and savings, to a more advanced industrial economy dependent upon impulsive buying and mass consumption. The world was indeed turned upside down. But not in the sense in which the world is turned upside down in madness, ecstasy, or carnival. The old social order was destroyed, but a new one was created based on profit and commodified pleasure.

8. Barbarism and Entertainment

In spite of certain limitations, James Twitchell's *Carnival Culture: The Trashing of Taste in America* is an especially useful guide to the history of popular culture since the age of the Enlightenment. Twitchell is a member of the school of "Cultural Studies" which by the 1990s had come to dominate theories of cultural criticism. Like Marxist critics before them, members of this school recognize that popular culture is a product of the rise of consumer markets and industrial techniques of mass production. Also like the Marxists, they understand that consumer markets do not educate or morally improve the masses. In fact, Twitchell describes popular culture as barbaric. But unlike the Marxists, the members of the school of Cultural Studies believe (1) that the market is determined from the bottom up by consumer demand rather than from the top down by the needs of capital, and (2) that consumer demand represents the democratic will of the people. Members of the school of Cultural Studies are adherents of what Thomas Frank (2000) calls market populism, the belief that in spending our dollars we are voting for products in a plebiscite that is more democratic than government could ever be. They believe that if the capitalist market has produced popular culture, then it has done so because that is what the people want. In responding to consumer demand the market is responding to the democratic will of the people.

But it is wrong to identify consumer demand with the democratic will of the people because democracy operates on the principle of one vote per person whereas the market operates on the principle of one "vote" per dollar, favoring the rich over the poor. Nor do consumer markets permit

the kind of rational, public deliberation that most democratic theorists have believed is necessary for democracy.

In a sense it is true that consumer markets merely respond to consumer demand. The essence of the act of consumption (and of entertainment as the act of consuming
information) is to satisfy desire. As such the act of consumption in a market economy is an act of voluntary exchange: money is exchanged for pleasure.

Nobody forces me to watch the latest Hollywood
blockbuster. And nobody forces the Hollywood movie producers to sell their product to me. We each get what we
want. The Hollywood movie producers get my money and
in exchange I get a pleasurable experience.

But, what people want is not necessarily the same as
what people would want if they were sufficiently well informed to know what their best interests were. The difference between these two is the basis for Rousseau's distinction between the "will of all" and the "general will." The
"will of all" is what the people actually desire. The "general
will" is what the people would want if the people were sufficiently well informed to know what their best interests
were. According to Rousseau, a legitimate democratic state
requires the consent of both the "will of all" and the "general will." In order to insure that the "will of all" coincides
with the "general will" a democratic state is obligated to
educate the public, in other words, to provide the public
with the means to determine what its best interests are.

Does the entertainment industry educate its "public"?
Do capitalist markets in general provide information to
consumers for the purpose of educating them? If they
don't, then market populism is false and consumer demand
may not be equated with the democratic will of the people.

Market populism is especially problematic when the
product being sold in the market is information. In the

classic liberal capitalist model of the marketplace, consumers bring their beliefs and desires with them prior to their market transactions. But what if the consumers' beliefs and desires are shaped by or originate in their market transactions? In that case buyers and sellers are no longer independent actors and we can no longer speak of a "voluntary exchange" between them. Instead, the consumer becomes an instrument of the marketplace. Thus, although it is true that consumers desire the products they consume, in the act of consuming those products their desires may change in ways they did not choose. This is especially true when the product being consumed is information, because information has the power to change consumers' beliefs and desires. Moreover, since information, like any other commodity, is produced for profit in a capitalist economy, consumers' beliefs and desires will be transformed not for the purpose of improving them but for the purpose of maximizing profits. For example, when a consumer grows up watching six hours of television per day, he is more likely to measure personal success in terms of the consumer lifestyle portrayed on television. The classic liberal assumption that consumers' beliefs and desires exist prior to market transactions may have been correct in the early nineteenth century when most consumers' beliefs and desires were shaped by traditional culture and information accounted for a very small fraction of the economy. But in today's post-industrial information economy the assumption no longer holds.

It is also important to remember that most consumers are workers. Although on the face of it consumers may appear to be free to choose, workers are not. Workers don't choose their place of employment with the same ease as consumers choose which movie they will watch. Nor do workers in the United States enjoy fundamental liberties such as freedom of speech in the workplace. If consumers wish to see the latest Hollywood blockbuster, it's in part because their desires have already been shaped by the alienated labor of the capitalist workplace where relationships are not genuinely free or democratic.

The identification of the market with democracy was characteristic of the triumphant capitalism of the 1990s in the wake of the fall of the Berlin Wall. It originates in theories of corporate management and served essentially as a cheerleader and public relations champion for capitalism in its moment of glory. It is not a product of a careful and balanced analysis of capitalism and democracy, and no such analysis is forthcoming in the school of Cultural Studies. However, between capitalism's cheerleaders and its critics we find common ground in the argument that popular culture is a product of the rise of consumer markets in the industrial and post-industrial age. It is this aspect of Twitchell's history of popular culture that I would like to make use of in this section.

In the eighteenth century Europe's population expanded, median age dropped, and literacy rates rose. In the nineteenth century mechanical printing presses and inexpensive paper made of wood pulp unleashed a tidal wave of printed matter to be consumed by the masses. In response to these developments, critics distinguished between high culture, popular culture and folk culture. High culture included the relatively small collection of classics held in most libraries prior to the eighteenth century. One of the distinguishing marks of high culture was the presence of a critical gatekeeper, a professional authority or expert who decided on the basis of some intellectual or aesthetic standard what would be admitted to the culture and what would not. High culture was originally the preserve of the wealthy, the literate and the clergy. Folk culture was produced non-commercially by anonymous amateurs and was passed informally by word of mouth. Folk culture was the oral culture of the common people of pre-industrial society. Popular culture was a commercial product of the industrial revolution and was manufactured using modern mechanical means of reproduction such as the printing press. As Twitchell (1992: 42-43) puts it, the products of popular culture are "formulaic, mass-produced, commercial, and the standard of acceptance is measured by the bottom line. Does it sell? Is it consumed? Its purpose is to entertain, not to enlighten."

So long as we remember that consumer demand must not be confused with the democratic will of the people, Twitchell's analysis is correct. According to Twitchell, between 1850 and 1950 high culture remained in the ascendancy. Since 1950, however, popular culture has gradually overtaken high culture and with it the roles of the author and gatekeeper. When the sole criteria for what gets published or broadcast is what sells, the author becomes an "agent of audience demand" and "the role of the gatekeeper, of priestly intercessionary, of a professional class of mediators vanishes." In a "transaction activated by audience attention, critics come after the entertainment, not before." (Twitchell, 1992: 268)

Twitchell describes the history of this struggle between high culture and popular culture in terms of the history of the concept of the "vulgar." Originally, Twitchell says, vulgarity was not a pejorative concept, but simply meant "of the common." The Vulgate, for instance, was the Latin version of the Bible for general circulation. But in the eighteenth century the concept of the vulgar was transformed to mean "something coarse and lacking in refinement." (Twitchell, 1992: 26) And with the rising tide of popular culture in the nineteenth century the concept of the vulgar came to mean something that threatened civilization itself. The Victorians coined the word 'mob' from the Latin *mobile vulgus* to mean 'the vulgar on the move,' and thereby linked the vulgar with mob violence. Popular culture was vulgar because it was common. But it was more than just common. It threatened civilization. According to a Victorian theory of social psychology, individuals lose their capacity for moral restraint and become capable of barbaric acts when they gather together in mobs. Victorians feared that popular culture could do the same. For the Victorians the psychology of mobs resembled the psychology of popular culture. Both organized people into a homogeneous mass in which individuality and self consciousness was lost. Both stirred up emotion and appealed to the senses while stifling intellectual and moral reflection. In both popular culture and mobs people seemed to lose their minds. According to Twitchell, the essence of the vulgar is that it aims to only excite the body. While pornography "may be one extreme of the vulgar, physical arousal is almost always involved in the experience. Generating laughter, tears, shivers, and swoons is what 'junk' usually strives for." (Twitchell, 1992: 54) By aiming only for pleasure, popular culture – like a mob – threatens to invert the social and psychic order by releasing the human body and its desires from moral and rational control.

Nowhere, says Twitchell, could the "vulgi" be more mobile than in America, where a populist culture and free enterprise nourished the entertainment industry. The Astor Place Riot of 1849 was, he believes, the opening salvo in the war between high culture and popular culture. In the Astor Place Riot of 1849 the aristocrats and the urban masses fought each other over which version of Shakespeare's plays would be performed. The aristocrats wanted the original performed while the mob wanted to improvise. William James spoke for the aristocrats when he said that the Astor Place Riot represented "the instinctive hostility of barbarism to culture." And until 1950 high culture held the upper hand. But according to Twitchell, by the latter half of the twentieth century the mass audience came to marginalize the elite.

In the view of members of the school of Cultural Studies the struggle between high culture and popular culture was a struggle for power between the upper classes and the people. Thus in their view the victory of popular culture in the latter part of the twentieth century represented not a victory for capitalism but a victory for democracy or the popular will of the people. That is why the Astor Place Riot occupies such an important place in Twitchell's narrative of the history of the struggle between high culture and popular culture. There the struggle between the two cultures was literally a struggle between two social classes.

Thomas Frank locates the origin of this view in Herbert Gans' 1974 book *Popular Culture and High Culture*. Gans rejected "the idea 'that popular culture is simply imposed on the audience from above,' that a malign culture industry is able to tell us what to think. In fact, he argues, audiences have the power to demand and receive, through the medium of the market, the culture of their choosing from the entertainment industry . . ." (Frank, 2000: 279-280) Cultural Studies in the late 1980s and 1990s picked up on this theme and developed it further while business leaders used it to legitimate the privatization and deregulation of the market. The free market thereby became linked with democracy and even with the struggle against racism. In 1988 historian Lawrence Levine argued in his book *High-brow/Lowbrow* that the consolidation of the high cultural canon in the nineteenth century was an instrument of racism and class oppression. He did this in part by portraying upper class men of the time as racists and snobs who used high culture to protect their class privileges and set themselves above the common people. While Twitchell holds popular culture in low esteem, he agrees with Levine that the rise of popular culture is a victory for democracy, and should be condoned for that reason. Thomas Frank (2000) argues differently. In his view popular culture is a business not a democratic forum. Its purpose is to generate profits not to satisfy the democratic will of the people. Hierarchies of taste and culture may or may not serve as instruments of social oppression, but when they do, popular culture may serve as an instrument of social oppression as much as or more than high culture.

Key to the notion of high culture in the nineteenth century was the role of the gatekeeper. It was the gatekeeper's duty to establish the canon, the original works of ideal beauty, and to divide them from what is vulgar. To cross the line separating the aesthetic from the vulgar was to challenge the authority of the gatekeeper.

During the nineteenth century classic literature was divided from popular literature. The Astor Place Riots were provoked by the mob's attempt to cross the line separating the authentic Shakespeare from the vulgar. Similarly, during the nineteenth century, as the high cultural canon was being consolidated, other areas of culture were divided between the aesthetic and the vulgar. At the beginning of the nineteenth century, according to Twitchell, opera was simultaneously common and elite, and only later came to be defined as part of the high cultural canon. Classical music wasn't separated off from popular music until the end of the nineteenth century.

Museum curators served as gatekeepers in the realm of art and separated the aesthetic from the vulgar by carefully controlling what entered their collections. Librarians served as gatekeepers in the realm of literature. Thus when the central branch of the Brooklyn Public Library opened in 1941 the following words were etched upon its facade:

> Here are enshrined the longing of great hearts and noble things that tower above the tide the magic word that winged wonder starts the garnered wisdom that never died.
>
> While men have wit to read and will to know, the door to learning is the open book.
>
> The library through the joining of municipal enterprise and private generosity offers to all the people perpetual and free access to the knowledge and the thought of all the ages.

In general, between 1850 and 1950, cultural authorities believed that in order to defend all areas of high culture, and consequently civilization itself, "the 'mobile vulgus' must be immobilized. We must memorialize the 'best that has been thought,' not the most popular, or the most entertaining, or even the most interesting. Needless to say, making these distinctions stick was the triumph of middle-class authority." (Twitchell, 1992: 32-33) Here again Twitchell and the school of Cultural Studies see the struggle between popular culture and high culture as a battle for control over social territory, so that the eventual victory of popular culture in the late twentieth century gets viewed as a democratic victory for the people. This view ignores the fact that the modern entertainment industry also depended upon huge sums of capital, not merely the willingness of the people to consume its products, and that unlike the symphony orchestras it was created primarily for the pur-

pose of making a profit, not for social or cultural better-
ment. But everyone agrees that by the latter half of the
twentieth century the barbarians had crashed the gates and
overrun the culture with vulgar amusements. In particular,
Twitchell's account of the history of the publishing industry
in the late twentieth century parallels what has happened
in public libraries and nicely illustrates the relationship between barbarism and the rise of consumer markets.
At least until the 1950s the printed word served as the
basis of the culture as a whole. Since the time of Aristotle
the West distinguished humans from animals by their ability to speak. Human culture was created by the Word and
the printing press allowed the Word to be efficiently pre-
served. Publishing was therefore a serious business and was
obligated to adhere to the highest standards. Publishers
served as gatekeepers, deciding what entered the culture
and what did not. As repositories of all that has been
printed, or at least of all printed material that is worth preserving, libraries defined the culture.

In the 1960s Herbert S. Bailey, director of Princeton
University Press, heard Charles Scribner say, "If books
become obsolete, I will make candles." Mr. Scribner didn't
say what he meant by that remark, but Mr. Bailey thought
what he had in mind was "that, although the electric light
has made candles obsolete, candle making today is a hun-
dred-million dollar industry—not large, but it casts a lovely
light. And after all, books are candles." (quoted in
Twitchell, 1992: 67) Books are candles because they enlighten, but they are also potentially incendiary. And that is
why publishers served as gatekeepers, protecting the culture by allowing light in and keeping fire out. In Umberto
Eco's novel *The Name of the Rose* Aristotle's treatise on comedy—on turning the world upside down, as in a carnival—
is kept hidden deep in the labyrinthine cells of a medieval

monastery. The librarian-monks consider this book so incendiary that if its ideas caught fire the entire Catholic world would be burnt to ashes. "The heart of its danger was that it celebrated the carnivalesque. It argued that the people should be able to decide what they want." (Twitchell, 1992: 70-71)

By the 1970s publishers used a more vulgar metaphor to describe books. Michael Korda, editor in chief of Simon & Schuster, said "We sell books, other people sell shoes. What's the difference? Publishing isn't the highest art." (quoted in Twitchell, 1992: 67) Selling books is like selling shoes. Whatever moves is published.

Books are no longer published because they enlighten but because they sell. Thus today, according to Twitchell, the librarian-monks can no longer keep Aristotle's treatise on comedy hidden. The world has become a carnival. The role of the gatekeeper and critic has been lost. And publishing is determined solely by audience or consumer demand.

The conflict between high culture and consumerism is not new. The Victorians sensed the danger of a culture driven by consumer demand in the nineteenth century when inexpensive pulp books were first manufactured. But in the publishing world the gatekeeper of ideas held sway over the merchandiser of books well into the second half of the twentieth century. What caused the gates to finally come crashing down, according to Twitchell (1992: 117), was "the introduction of the paperback book and the conglomeration of the entertainment industry in the 1970s and 1980s."

In 1939 DeGraff introduced not only the paperback book but a new way of merchandising them. He sold paperback books like shoes, aiming to sell as many as possible. He utilized the same distribution chains as magazines, selling them in drugstores and newstands rather than bookstores. Soon publishers were offering major retail chains such as Woolworth and K-mart a deep 45 percent discount on books. The next logical step would have been for the publishers to move into the retail business themselves and own the outlets, as the movie studios had owned theaters prior to the 1950s. But due to concerns about anti-trust violations the publishers could not make this move. Instead, the bookstores conglomerated with merchandisers. Waldenbooks, for example, became a subsidiary of K-mart.

Not surprisingly, given who owns them, the chain bookstores operate like a retail business. Books are arranged according to their potential to generate sales revenues and are attractively displayed to catch shoppers' attention. Muzak plays in the background. Sales people are trained in customer service but know nothing about books. Book purchasing is handled in the same way a retail business manages its inventory. There's no need for a critical gatekeeper who selects books on the basis of qualitative judgements. In fact there's no need for human intervention in the book ordering process at all. That can be done by a machine. Electronic cash registers can automatically tabulate inventory and issue lists of titles to be reordered. "Shocking as it would seem to Charles A. Scribner and his sons, the chief monk in publishing is a middle-level executive at a subsidiary of the K-mart corporation looking at small blinking numbers on a computer screen. 'Get me some more Danielle Steel and Stephen King,' he says . . ." (Twitchell, 1992: 102)

As it turns out, what these electronic inventory systems are ordering is increasingly violent and anti-social. Violence sells. Since the stated mission of public libraries generally includes some reference to education or the public interest, they have reason to be more judicious in their selection of books. But as the cost of computer technology drops and the distinction between the public and private realm deteriorates further, libraries are increasingly utilizing the same technology to order books as the chain bookstores, and doing away with librarians (those quiet folks who know books) in the process.

While the bookstores were bought up by retail businesses, the publishing houses were absorbed into giant entertainment conglomerates. The printed word has consequently been transformed from a medium of education and high culture into a form of entertainment. But entertainment is a form of consumption, and consumer products are produced for profit. Thus, "book publishers are behaving more like movie distributors: making their decisions about profitability first, and last: 'Don't tell us how good it is,' they say. 'Tell us who is going to buy it.'" (Twitchell, 1992: 129)

According to Gerald Howard, an editor at W. W. Norton, the publishing industry is torn between two competing functions: "the higher-minded and more vocally trumpeted *mission civilisatrice* to instruct and edify and uplift the reading public and the less loudly advertised but in the nature of things, more consistently compelling *mission commerciale* to separate the consumer from his cash." (quoted in Twitchell, 1992: 116) Before the absorption of the publishing industry into the entertainment conglomerates the balance tilted in favor of the *mission civilisatrice*. Henry Holt, for example, condemned the *mission commerciale* on the grounds that it represented an "abandonment of morals and the degradation of activities to a lowered level of purpose" and that "pandering to a vulgar popular taste" was the book publishing counterpart to "yellow" journalism (quoted in Twitchell, 1992: 111-112). Even in magazine publishing Luce, the founder of *Time*, brought a missionary zeal to his work and spoke of his magazine in grandiose terms as "a weekly record of our civilization." But entertainment strives merely to please the audience in exchange for its cash. So, since publishing was absorbed by the entertainment conglomerates, the balance has shifted towards the *mission commerciale.* Pandering, Twitchell concludes, has become the norm. Publishers no longer seek to edify their readers. And libraries are not far behind.

A particularly clear example of pandering in the publishing industry can be found in public journalism, a way of practicing journalism that took hold of newspaper publishing during the booming "New Economy" era of the 1990s. Public journalism was especially well received by the Gannet newspaper chain that includes *USA Today.* In essence, public journalism rejects the educational or critical role of newspaper writers and editors, asserting instead that the purpose of a newspaper is to voice the opinions of its readers. "The key to solving journalism's problems, its leaders maintained, was to understand editing as customer service." (Frank, 2000: 318) To achieve this end public journalism sets editorial policy according to the same sort of marketing research that one would use to sell hamburgers or cans of soda. Polls, demographic surveys and focus groups are conducted to test audience response, and editorial policy is set accordingly within the constraints of profit and loss calculations.

Similarly, during the 1990s, when FM radio was absorbed into the great infotainment conglomerates, programming decisions were typically made by testing the reaction to various songs of a sampling of people from advertisers' target population. The songs that got aired by this process were those which were most familiar or which offended the fewest listeners—in other words, the lowest common denominator of the target consumer group.

Market populism teaches us intellectual humility in the face of the market. New Economy corporate management gurus such as Peter Senge, for example, insisted that we must do what the market tells us to do and give up our attempt to understand or control it. Since the market is an expression of the will of the people, intellectual humility in the face of the market is, according to Peter Senge, an expression of faith in the people (Frank, 2000: 196). Attempts to understand or control the market, in this view, are elitist, and are as doomed to fail as attempts to control acts of nature.

Public journalism in turn merely brought the ideology of market populism and its inherent anti-intellectualism into the field of journalism. The purpose of journalism is not to educate the public but to give consumers what they want. In other words, to pander.

Indeed according to Frank (2000: 198), anti-intellectualism is found throughout New Economy thought: "In nearly every field we will examine, market populists were advising Americans to drop their futile efforts to figure the world out and to submit humbly to the will of the market." The anti-intellectualism of the era manifested itself in the job market for professionals whose mission is to educate or understand human society. Critical editors and investigative reporters were laid off. Newly minted Ph.D.'s in the humanities and social sciences faced the worst job market in academic history. But the MBA remained a ticket to success.

Much of the intellectual humility of market populism is ultimately derived from the work of F. A. Hayek and Milton Friedman. Hayek (1944) argued that the market is a complex natural phenomenon unamenable to conscious human control. In a free (unregulated) market the unintended effects of countless independent consumer decisions will produce the most desirable outcome. But any attempt to consciously control the economy is bound to fail because the market is much too complex for human reason to ever grasp. For Hayek the important implication of his theory of the market is that the economy cannot and must not be centrally planned by the state or any other group of conscious actors no matter how rational or well intentioned they may be.

However, aside from the question as to whether Hayek's radical libertarian economic theories are correct or not, they had little real relevance to what was happening in the New Economy of the 1990s other than to provide rhetorical support for privatization and deregulation that favored business, because the New Economy was not by any stretch of the imagination a free or competitive market. Government continued to account for anywhere from twenty five to over fifty percent of the Gross Domestic Product of developed nations, while the private sector consolidated into giant transnational conglomerates. The transnational corporations operated as top-down command and control economies with no credible pretense to being democratic organizations while their revenues often exceeded that of small nation states.

For all its pretenses to serving democracy, the Gannet newspaper chain was hardly a democratic institution. Gannet gave its readers what they wanted, at least superficially, but only if they were the readers its advertisers wanted to reach. Hayek may have rejected the possibility of centralized control of large scale organizations, but that is exactly what Gannet was. Public journalism may have praised the wisdom of the common people, but Gannet failed to give its own employees decent wages and working conditions. In fact, in 1998 Linda Foley, president of the Newspaper Guild, told Thomas Frank that "Gannet is among the most anti-union companies that we deal with." (quoted in Frank, 2000: 325) The News Museum opened by Gannett in 1997 documents the history of feminism, the civil rights movement and the struggle for free speech, but makes no mention at all of labor history.

The elitism that market populism rails against is not the elitism of money and power, but the elitism of high culture. Thus Al Neuhart, the founder of *USA Today*, has no difficulty accepting a CEO's salary while accusing journalists of being undemocratic and elitist if they wish to make editorial decisions on the basis of critical standards. Market populism gives us the worst of both worlds: extreme economic and political injustice combined with cultural nihilism.

9. From Citizen to Consumer

The 1920s witnessed a dramatic boom in consumer markets as the techniques of mass production were perfected. "Fordism" required that workers be given a sufficient wage to consume the products of their labor in order to stimulate higher levels of production and profits. Interrupted by the Great Depression, the expansion of mass consumer markets resumed after the Second World War with the construction of the suburbs, the growth of the automobile industry, and the introduction of television. By the 1990s an extreme form of consumer capitalism had appeared which almost completely replaced the citizen with the consumer. The suburbs privatized what had been public spaces in urban settings. These newly privatized spaces were in turn segmented by socio-economic status. Consequently the notion of the public good was progressively narrowed, until the nation splintered into various identity groups competing for private goods. Politicians representing business interests took advantage of the consumerization of American society by promoting privatization and deregulation while paying homage to multiculturalism. As business recovered in the postwar years from the loss of credibility it had suffered during the Great Depression, and as the pursuit of private consumer goods became the primary preoccupation of most Americans, there was increasing pressure to either privatize government services or to model them on business practices. Government itself came to be viewed as a customer service.

Lizabeth Cohen (2003) offers a particularly good analysis of the privatization and segmentation of the public domain in postwar America. She explains how federal dollars for home mortgages during the postwar years inequitably favored single family houses in homogeneous white, middle class areas such as Nassau County in Long Island and suburban New Jersey, while rural or inner city areas received practically nothing. Residents of Hudson County, north of New York City, "received only $12 of mortgage insurance per capita, the second lowest total in the nation after the Bronx, in sharp contrast to Nassau County, home of suburban Levittown and Garden City, where residents had received $601 per capita." (Cohen, 2003: 205) Federally financed suburban communities had fewer public spaces than older urban neighborhoods and were more segmented by socio-economic class. The cost of housing served to exclude the poor and working class from suburban developments while racism added to the obstacles faced by blacks. As white, middle class Americans retreated behind white picket fences, their conception of the public good narrowed. The inequities of the housing market produced inequities in public services such as schools and libraries that were funded by local property taxes. By the 1990s there were attempts to privatize schools through voucher programs. Even a few libraries were privatized, and those that weren't outsourced more of their work to private vendors.

Cities are distinguished from suburbs by streets and sidewalks where pedestrians cross paths with others from all walks of life. Cities have traditionally hosted an array of public and private spaces where people from across the social spectrum may meet and gather, such as saloons, cafes, libraries, bookstores, clubs, lecture halls, parks and museums. Suburbs on the other hand offer relatively few public spaces, and private spaces are segmented by economic status. There are often no sidewalks. People travel in automobiles from one private space to another. In the 1990s many of those automobiles were SUVs or had tinted windshields. People adopted a defensive posture toward others in public spaces. And a military personnel carrier, the Humvee, was sold as the ultimate SUV. While it was still possible to see others on city streets, it was possible to walk down a suburban street and not see another living soul.

Another distinguishing feature of the suburb is the shopping mall. City shopping districts or commercial avenues are public spaces where citizens enjoy all civil rights and engage in other activities besides shopping such as working or attending religious services. Shopping malls are private spaces where consumers enjoy restricted rights at the discretion of mall owners and managers. Protesters, for example, have no legally guaranteed right to express their opinions in shopping malls. "Overall," Cohen (2003: 286) concludes, "an important shift from one kind of social order to another took place between 1950 and 1980, with major consequences for Americans. A free commercial market attached to a relatively free public space (for whites) underwent a transformation to a more regulated commercial marketplace (where mall management controlled access, favoring, for example, chains over independents) and a more circumscribed public sphere of limited rights."

Many other observers have commented on the danger of shopping malls. Benjamin Barber attributes the commercialization of everyday life to the development of shopping malls. "The isolation of commercial space from every other kind of public space hinted at by the world's fairs and certified by mall development has allowed commercial consumption to dominate public space, transforming every other human activity into a variation of buying and selling." (Barber, 1995: 130) Carole Rifkind complains that the "mall is only one component of the ongoing convulsive privatization of the public realm." She warns us not to "pretend, as some have, that malls will eventually mature into true community centers. And let's hope we'll wake up sometime soon and realize that citizenship is, after all, more important than consumerism." (in Washburn, 1996: 267-268)

We saw above how the development of democracy depended upon the development of a reasoning public and how this public was fostered by distinctive settings and media from scientific societies, literary salons, Masonic lodges, and coffeehouses to publishing houses, libraries and the daily newspaper. These settings and media were, Poggi (1978: 81) said, "public in being accessible to all interested comers, or at least to all those possessing appropriate, objectively ascertainable qualifications, such as learning, technical competence, relevant information, persuasive eloquence, creative imagination, and capacity for critical judgment." Jurgen Habermas, too, believed that the development of democracy in the eighteenth and nineteenth centuries depended upon a rational public sphere sustained by accessible urban spaces. For these reasons Cohen (2003: 289) fears that the "commercializing, privatizing, and segmenting of physical gathering places that has resulted from allowing the unfettered pursuit of profits to dictate a new metropolitan landscape has made more precarious the shared public sphere upon which democracy depends."

Suburbanization was a major cause of consumerism and the decline of a shared public sphere in American life in the second half of the twentieth century. Developments in marketing and advertising were another major cause. These in turn were related to developments in the technology and economics of mass production.

During the 1920s the technology of mass production and the size of consumer markets were such that cost per unit was lowest when the greatest number of items of the same type were produced. The original Model T Ford, for example, came in only one color: black. Such a means of production fitted well with Taylor's theories of scientific management and with the large scale, centralized bureaucratic corporations of that age. A uniform system of bureaucratic rules could be used to manage a large corporation just as a uniform production process could be used to produce many items of the same type. The apogee of this system occurred in the 1950s. At that point mass markets began to become saturated with uniform products and had grown larger than economies of scale required. For example, the growth of the suburbs increased the demand for automobiles beyond the point where it was necessary to produce only black Model T Fords to achieve the greatest economy of scale. In order to increase production and profits it was necessary not to expand markets for uniform products further, but rather to divide the mass market into parts for which different products could be produced. Thus, for example, different models of automobiles could be produced for different segments of the population.

Often the differences between products were superficial. During the 1950s and 1960s automobile bodies were changed annually with great fanfare, while the underlying chassis and drive train remained relatively unchanged. The image of the automobiles coming out of Detroit changed greatly as wings sprouted on tailgates, but the substance was little changed. To make the most of these superficial changes advertisers invested these images with added meaning. One image might symbolize conservative stability while another might symbolize youthful daring. By investing different images with different meanings, advertisers were able to market superficially different products to different segments of the population.

Limiting further profit growth was not the only concern voiced in the 1950s about scientifically managed bureaucracies and the mass production of uniform products.
Social commentators complained that American society
was becoming too conformist. An ethic of diversity subse-
quently developed which spawned a rebellious youth culture and allowed various ethnic groups to create unique
identities. Politicians learned to cater to these developments by tailoring their message to different segments of
the population, mimicking the market segmentation practiced by advertisers.

In 1956 retired adman John G. Schneider published a
best-selling novel titled *The Golden Kazoo* in which he sati-
rized the use of mass marketing techniques in political election campaigns. The novel follows the attempts of a Madison Avenue advertising executive, Blade Reade, to sell a
Republican candidate for the presidency to the public.
Blade packages his candidate for television audiences as a
"*simple* picture—a beautiful, powerful, appealing but simple
picture" aimed at what Blade calls "a real, low-down Lowest Common Denominator" determined by scientific polls.
However, what "Schneider could not predict in 1956,"
Cohen explains, "was that the advent of market segmentation later that decade would change the rules of the game
for political marketing, as it had for product marketing,
pushing campaigns and electioneering away from selling to
Blade Reade's 'Lowest Common Denominator' mass market toward crafting special messages for distinctive segments about whom more and more was becoming known
through increasingly sophisticated polling." (Cohen, 2003:
336) John F. Kennedy was the first presidential candidate
to utilize techniques of market segmentation. The presidential campaign of 1960 is noteworthy, Cohen says, "for
Kennedy's new attention to voter segments, rather than

solely to the mass of Americans as Eisenhower had. Kennedy hired Louis Harris to do private state-level polling for him and used his findings to tailor his messages, such as on civil rights, to the occasion of his speechmaking." (Cohen, 2003: 336) Kennedy also dispatched his brother-in-law Sargent Shriver to set up special units of the Democratic National Committee to devise strategies for reaching out to various special interest groups, such as ethnic groups, senior citizens, labor, businessmen and farmers.

Just as segmented consumers seek products that satisfy their special tastes and desires, segmented voters seek political candidates who will satisfy their special needs and interests. Therefore the effect of market segmentation in political campaigns is to discourage discussion of a common good. But once the notion of a common good is lost the political arena becomes a battleground for competing private interests similar to the commercial marketplace. We are a short step away from equating democracy with markets and citizens with consumers. Increasingly toward the end of the twentieth century, citizens "were bringing market expectations to their appraisals of the government itself, judging it and its policies by the personal benefits they, as segmented purchasers as citizens, derived from them." (Cohen, 2003: 344)

Every presidential administration since Gerald Ford's defended its efforts toward privatization and deregulation as improving consumer interest while at the same time reversing older Keynesian policies that stimulated consumer demand. In 1993 the Clinton-Gore administration published its National Performance Review Report titled *From Red Tape to Results: Creating a Government that Works Better and Costs Less.* "The report listed among its top goals 'putting customers first,' proposing a new-style government modeled after the efficient retail business: 'Effective, entrepreneurial governments insist on customer satisfaction. They listen carefully to their customers—using surveys, focus groups, and the like. They restructure their basic operations to meet customers' needs. And they use market dynamics such as competition and customer choice to create incentives that drive their employees to put customers first.'" (Cohen, 2003: 396) In 1995 Vice President Gore advocated further privatization of postal services to improve customer service, while during the 1996 presidential campaign Republican candidate Robert Dole promised students and their parents a "consumer's warranty" from the nation's public schools. In 2002 the Bush administration announced its intention to place half the federal civilian work force up for competition from private contractors in order to "get the best deal for taxpayers and to ensure the highest level of government services" and to "create a market-based government unafraid of competition, innovation and choice" (Stevenson, 2002). As "the market relationship became the template for the citizen's connection to government," public spirited citizens were as a consequence replaced by "self-interested government consumers," who were "encouraged to bring a consumer mentality to their relations with government, judging public services and tax assessments much like other purchased goods, by the personal benefits they derived from them." (Cohen, 2003: 397)

If nobody noticed that democracy had been replaced by capitalism that may be because, according to the prevailing ideology of market populism, capitalism is democratic. Thomas Frank cites the curious tendency for conservatives in the mid-1990s to describe the operations of government in the language of business. For example, journalist John Fund wrote "that if government 'were a consumer product on a store shelf, it would be removed for being defective and sued for false advertising.' Give the people of America *real* democracy—the democracy of the competitive marketplace: 'They want to be treated as customers, not constituents.'" (Frank, 2000: 48) In the 1990s the customer service model could be taken to truly ridiculous lengths. In "Woolly Pulpit" Hanna Rosin quotes a pastor who seeks to adopt the customer service model. "'People think of the church as a draconian thing of the past, with big towers and iron gates and frocked people who do weird things and speak a language no one understands,' the pastor explains. 'We get the message out that we are relevant,' as relevant as, say, your local mall. 'The shopping center makes you feel comfortable,' clarifies Assistant Pastor Frank Bouts. 'We want our church to be equally as customer-service oriented, or equally sensitive to the needs of all the seekers, all the first-time visitors who come here.'" (in Washburn, 1996: 38) In New York City Police Commissioner Bernard B. Kerik announced in 2001 that the police would "be expected to use a customer service model, similar to that used by Wal-Mart Stores, aimed at making precinct station houses more businesslike and accessible. To that end, officers will be assigned to greet people as they walk through station house doors." The plan was intended to improve community relations in the wake of incidents such as the station house torture of Abner Louima in 1997 and the shooting of Amadou Diallo in 1999 (Rashbaum, 2001).

When citizens become consumers election campaigns become advertisements and politicians become entertainers. That is literally what happened in 2003 when Arnold Schwarzenegger was elected Governor of California. Although most Americans hardly noticed, the European press was quick to recognize what had happened. Mr. Schwarzenegger's campaign was all image and no substance. He refused to take a stand on the issues, relying instead on his popularity as an entertainment celebrity. "Schwarzenegger replaces politics with entertainment— this is his primary sin," the German daily Suddeutsche Zeitung said. "The man lets himself be wrapped up for the voters as a governor, without allowing them to take a look inside the package. He reduced the campaign to the secret motto: vote for me because I'm famous." (quoted in Bernstein, 2003)

10. Democracy, the Public Good and the Postmodern Information Economy

We have seen that modern democracy as originally conceived is sustained by citizens who engage in rational deliberation with one another on the nature of the public or common good. Market economies, however, allow us to only individually choose private goods. For this reason they tend to promote subjective theories of truth and value. And, when markets become mediums for the exchange of information, they do so in order to satisfy consumer demand and generate profits, not to edify or educate the public. Information traded in a market is entertainment. Information markets therefore do a poor job of fostering a rational public conversation because by their very nature they tend to undermine both reason and the public sphere. And since democracy requires a rational public sphere, information markets tend to undermine democracy, too.

In the wake of the fall of the Berlin wall, politicians and business leaders in the West have used the concepts of democracy and the market interchangeably, as if they meant the same thing. This is the essence of the ideology of market populism that Thomas Frank (2000) exposed in *One Market Under God*. But democracy is not the same as the market. Not only are there examples of capitalist societies that do not enjoy democratic systems of governance, but democracy often defends public goods such as the environment or full employment at the expense of private commercial interests. And while postmodern consumer capitalism attempts to manipulate consumers' needs and desires in what Benjamin Barber (1995) calls the "infotainment telesector," democracy thrives when citizens engage in rational dialogue with one another in the public domain. The infotainment telesector includes the industries of advertising, entertainment, computer software and telecommunications. While the USA imports more and more manufacturing goods from abroad, creating an ever larger trade deficit, a large portion of that trade deficit is offset by net exports from the infotainment telesector. That's why the infotainment telesector was a darling of business leaders and politicians during the booming New Economy era of the 1990s. Their vision was of an American economy that produced "brands" and "symbols" while the rest of the world produced material goods for us. Tony Blair across the Atlantic shared a similar vision for his nation. Americans were told that they would be compensated for the loss of manufacturing jobs with good paying jobs in the information economy. But by 2003, when large numbers of information processing jobs began to get outsourced to India and China, that claim became much less credible (Herbert, 2003). The infotainment telesector is a transnational system that is indifferent to public goods such as full employment.

The infotainment telesector has fundamentally altered the way that capitalism operates because it alters the relationship between symbol and reality, consumer demand and supply, use value and exchange value. Whereas classic liberal capitalism presupposed that the elements of each of these binary pairs was independent of the other, the postmodern information economy deconstructs the opposition between them. For example, when what we are consuming is as much meaning as reality, symbols are no longer inferior to reality. Brands such as Coca Cola, Marlboro, KFC, McDonald's, Nike, Levi's, Pepsi, and Wrigley are selling symbols of an American lifestyle as much as material goods. When Madison Avenue invests a certain automobile design with the meaning of rugged outdoor adventures, driving becomes as much a symbolic wilderness excursion as a way to get from one place to another. Material goods, says Barber (1995: 59), "are increasingly associated with or defined by the symbolic interactions that belong to the service sector in its postmodern, virtual economy manifestations... hard consumer goods are increasingly becoming associated with soft technologies rooted in information, entertainment, and lifestyle." The relationship between consumer demand and supply is altered when demand can be shaped by the infotainment telesector to meet supply. "The ancient capitalist economy in which products are manufactured and sold for profit to meet the demand of consumers who make their unmediated needs known through the market is gradually yielding to a postmodern capitalist economy in which needs are manufactured to meet the supply of producers who make their unmediated products marketable through promotion, spin, packaging, and advertising." (Barber, 1995: 59) Use value can no longer be defined independently of exchange value when information is produced to alter our perception of utility in order to satisfy the capitalist imperative to increase exchange value or generate profits. Each of these oppositions allowed classic liberal economists such as John Stuart Mill to believe that the market could serve a higher moral purpose. Without them we enter a new era in which capital serves no higher purpose than itself.

No less a capitalist than George Soros, who made billions in world currency markets, believes that this extreme form of postmodern capitalism is a threat not only to humanity but to itself. Soros (1997) appeals to Hegel's dialectical conception of history according to which any idea taken to an extreme turns into its opposite. Soros warns that this could happen to liberal capitalism unless a delib-

erate effort is made to prevent it. The weak link in classic
economic theory according to Soros is that it does not account for reflexivity. This is due to the fact that classic economic theory was based on Newtonian mechanics. In
Newtonian mechanics the object of knowledge is not altered by the act of knowing it. In quantum physics, on the
other hand, Heisenberg's uncertainty principle tells us that
the object of knowledge is altered by the act of knowing it,
or at least of measuring it. In the human sciences, including
economics and finance, the object of study is also altered
by the act of knowing it, because the object of knowledge is
ourselves. Thus there is a feedback loop uniting the knower
with the known. This feedback loop or reflexivity makes for
an unstable and unpredictable system.

> The condition that supply and demand are inde-
> pendently given cannot be reconciled with reality,
> at least as far as financial markets are concerned—
> and financial markets play a crucial role in the al-
> location of resources. Buyers and sellers in financial
> markets seek to discount a future that depends on
> their own decisions. The shape of the supply and
> demand curves cannot be taken as given because
> both of them incorporate expectations about
> events that are shaped by those expectations.
> There is a two-way feedback mechanism between
> the market participants' thinking and the situation
> they think about—"reflexivity."
>
> Economic theory has managed to create an artifi-
> cial world in which the participants' preferences
> and the opportunities confronting participants are
> independent of each other, and prices tend toward
> an equilibrium that brings the two forces into bal-
> ance. But in financial markets prices are not
> merely the passive reflection of independently

given demand and supply; they also play an active role in shaping those preferences and opportunities. This reflexive interaction renders financial markets inherently unstable. Laissez-faire ideology denies the instability and opposes any form of government intervention aimed at preserving stability. History has shown that financial markets do break down, causing economic depression and social unrest. (Soros, 1997)

Soros believes that government should regulate the market but acknowledges that regulations can introduce instabilities of their own. In Soros' view, which is derived from Karl Popper's notion of the "Open Society," the solution is to take a trial and error approach and be prepared to change the regulations as needed depending on outcomes.

Of even more relevance to democracy and the public good than what Soros has to say about financial markets, however, is what he has to say about values. Besides taking supply and demand as givens, classic economic theory took people's values and preferences as given. However, as we have seen, especially in a postmodern information economy, use value is not independent of exchange value. There is a reflexive relationship between them that makes them inherently unstable. Up through the Victorian era, perhaps, it could be assumed that people brought values with them prior to their market transactions. At the time economic theory was born, there were important spheres of activity outside the reach of the commercial marketplace. At the time economic theory was born, the market had not grown so powerful or existed for so long as to overtake values rooted in tradition, religion and culture. In the past century however the market has imposed its own values on us as exchange value has gradually overtaken use value, making money the measure of all value.

There has been an ongoing conflict between market values and other, more traditional value systems, which has aroused strong passions and antagonisms. As the market mechanism has extended its sway, the fiction that people act on the basis of a given set of nonmarket values has become progressively more difficult to maintain. Advertising, marketing, even packaging, aim at shaping people's preferences rather than, as laissez-faire theory holds, merely responding to them. Unsure of what they stand for, people increasingly rely on money as the criterion of value. What is more expensive is considered better. The value of a work of art can be judged by the price it fetches. People deserve respect and admiration because they are rich. What used to be a medium of exchange has usurped the place of fundamental values, reversing the relationship postulated by economic theory. What used to be professions have turned into businesses. The cult of success has replaced belief in principles. Society has lost its anchor. (Soros, 1997)

What is this anchor of which Soros speaks? In traditional metaphysics reality is a great chain of moral purposes anchored in God who is the highest good. Words play off against one another in a complex web of metaphor and metonym, but their meaning is ultimately anchored in the Real, to which they refer. When Nietzsche declared the death of God he meant to announce the end of both traditional metaphysics and a theory of language anchored in the Real. Nietzsche predicted that following the death of God the West would endure a period of nihilism until a new system of values could be created. The postmodern information age is that period of nihilism.

Money has no other use than to be exchanged for other objects of value. Money is pure exchange value. But in general, objects have many other values attached to them. A beautiful painting, for example, may fetch a handsome price on the market, but it is also beautiful. A house may be worth a great deal of money, but it also provides shelter. Nor is an object's exchange value necessarily an accurate measure of its other values. In fact it is the difference between an object's use value and its exchange value that motivates its exchange. If I barter a hen for a rooster it's because the rooster has greater use to me than the hen, even though they have the same exchange value.

Capital has no other use than to increase exchange value or generate profits. Capital is money used to make more money ad infinitum without end. Insofar as production is determined by capital, its only purpose is to make more money. But capital is constrained by consumer demand. Consumers purchase products because they believe their use value is greater than their exchange value. Thus capital must produce useful objects as a means to increase exchange value. Capital therefore has an interest in shaping consumers' perceptions of what is useful. To the extent that it succeeds in doing so, use value is reduced to exchange value and production takes place only to make more money, not to accomplish any other good. The infotainment telesector provides capital with a powerful means of shaping consumers' perceptions of what is useful, because information alters people's preferences. Thus the information economy detaches production from any final good.

Just as classic liberal economics assumed that people brought values with them prior to their market transactions, so too did traditional metaphysics assume that people brought meaning with them prior to their use of language.

For example, the word 'triangle' has a meaning that is independent of the word 'triangle.' The meaning of the word 'triangle' is not created by our use of the word. Rather we use the word 'triangle' to express and refer to what we already understand to be a triangle. If we spelled the word 'triangle' differently its meaning would not automatically change. If we used a different font style when typing or printing the word 'triangle' its meaning would not change. The actual sounds or marks we use to indicate words are arbitrary conventions. We could change each letter of the alphabet and convey the same meanings if we had a code that could translate one set of letters into the other. All that would be required is that the number of different letters remain the same, because the sole function of a letter is to mark its difference from other letters. A string of letters or sounds or other characters that conveys a meaning is a "signifier." The word 'triangle' is a signifier. Its meaning is a "signified." Together the signifier and the signified form the "sign" which refers to a real or imaginary object, the "referent."

Information resides in the differences between signifiers and their sequence. The same information can be transmitted by a different set of signifiers so long as their number and sequence remains the same. Computers process information as a string of 1s and 0s or high and low voltage levels. But a code exists that can be used to translate certain strings of 1s and 0s into the letters of the alphabet. Thus the same information can be transmitted by a string of 1s and 0s as by a string of letters. However, information is not the same as meaning. Information merely allows us to encode meaning. A computer does not contain the meaning of the word 'triangle,' it merely contains a string of high and low voltage levels which when decoded by a human being mean what we mean by the word 'triangle.' Signifiers and signifieds exist on two parallel planes, just as exchange value and use value did in classic liberal economics. Signifiers are defined horizontally by their differences from other signifiers, but vertically by their meaning and the referent to which they refer. Just as the extreme capitalist economy reduces use value to exchange value, so does the postmodern information economy reduce meaning and knowledge to mere information. The extreme capitalist economy is an endless exchange of money and commodities that never comes to rest in any final use value. The value of any commodity in an extreme capitalist economy is not given by its vertical relation to its use value, but rather by its horizontal relation to money and other commodities with which it might be exchanged. The postmodern information economy is an endless exchange of signifiers that never comes to rest in the referent. The significance of any signifier in the postmodern information economy is not given by its vertical relation to the referent, but rather by its horizontal relation to other signifiers. Its significance is that it is different than other signifiers. Otherwise it could not be used to transmit information. As a commodity in a market it has an exchange value equal to its price. For producers its use value is profit. For consumers information may be consumed for the purpose of education or edification, but in the postmodern information economy information is consumed much more often for the purpose of pleasure only, because the postmodern "infotainment telesector" produces information in the form of entertainment, and entertainment is information that is consumed only for pleasure. Thus the signified and its referent—the ideational and epistemic content of language—is of little significance in a postmodern information economy. Instead of operating as a carrier of symbolic meaning, language operates at the level of the signifier as a physical force that causes pleasurable sensations and emotions in consumers. We do not so much read or interpret language in a postmodern information economy as we plug into it or engage gears with it. In fact, words are of secondary importance to pictures in the infotainment economy because pictures have more immediate physical effects than words. We are living in an epoch in which visual images have replaced words as the primary means of human communication. But Barber (1995) is rightly skeptical that such images can transmit knowledge.

Before the development of the postmodern information economy, capitalism "had to capture political institutions and elites in order to control politics, philosophy, and religion so that through them it could nurture an ideology conducive to its profits. Today it manufactures as among its chief and most profitable products that very ideology itself." (Barber, 1995: 77) It is an ideology embedded in the medium as well as the message. "How," Barber asks, "can the public be represented by markets that privilege individual consumption, taken consumer by consumer, but have no way of representing public goods—what individuals share and thus what makes them more than consumers? Where are the market incentives to protect public interests?" (Barber, 1995: 86) The ideology represented by consumer markets is an ideology of "fun" that recognizes no workers, only consumers; no collective will, only independent consumer choices; no class interests, only a global pop culture. But it is not precisely correct to say that the market represents an ideology at all. The market is indifferent to our ideas. It acts instead to affect our behavior and emotional responses. How could a public sphere of abstract reasoning possibly be maintained by a market that communicates primarily by pictures to produce the most immediate physical effects on consumers? "The abstraction of language is superseded by the literalness of pictures—at a yet to be determined cost to imagination, which languishes as its work is done for it; to community, which is bound together by words; and to public goods, which demand the interactive deliberation of rational choices armed with literacy." (Barber, 1995: 89) The infotainment telesector is a threat not only to democracy and the public domain, but to reason itself.

Hollywood is one of America's most successful industries—so successful, in fact, that it has squelched domestic filmmaking in almost every other nation in the world. But Hollywood is not just one among many industries. Hollywood produces the images that shape all consumer behavior. Hollywood films "have the status of amusements but they are likely to inspire a vision of life and to affect habits and attitudes. Hollywood is McWorld's storyteller. . . [and McWorld is] an entertainment shopping experience that brings together malls, multiplex movie theaters, theme parks, spectator sports arenas, fast-food chains (with their endless movie tie-ins), and television (with its burgeoning shopping networks) into a single vast enterprise that, on the way to maximizing its profits, transforms human beings." (Barber, 1995: 97) Now that the entertainment industry has been consolidated into a few huge conglomerates, Hollywood dominates other, less profitable media industries, including publishing. Most of the profits in the publishing industry are generated by the .008% of all the books in print that are on the bestseller list at any one time (Twitchell, 1992: 81). But even the profits generated from a best-selling book are minor in comparison to the profits to be made from a blockbuster movie. And so, since the publishing houses are owned by the same conglomerates that own the movie studios, there is enormous incentive not

only to produce a few best-selling books, but also to produce best-selling books that can be made into movies. Consequently, according to Barber (1995: 120), when the how-
to books were removed from the *New York Times* bestseller
list, they were quickly replaced by genre novels designed to
be made into movies. "Paramount, even though it owns
Simon & Schuster, cannot really afford to have people read
books unless they are reading novelizations of Paramount
movies." (Barber, 1995: 116)

By reducing culture to pictorial entertainment and citizens to isolated individual consumers, the infotainment
telesector precludes the possibility of a rational public
sphere. There can be no public good for isolated individual
consumers. Nor can consumers reason abstractly or deliberate with one another if their primary source of information is pictorial and the only public space in which they can
meet with one another is the local mall. Democracy requires rational deliberation. But only words enable citizens
to deliberate with one another or reason abstractly. Thus,
without rational deliberation there can be consumer
choice. But there can be no democracy. The public library
offers an obvious remedy for these ills, but as government
abandons its responsibility to educate citizens for democracy in favor of providing better customer service, the public library has fallen into the clutches of the postmodern
information economy, too.

Earlier in the twentieth century government had not
yet abandoned its responsibility to promote civic education. In 1934 the Federal Communications Commission
was established to "encourage the larger and more effective
uses of radio in the public interest." The trend toward privatization and deregulation that began almost thirty years
ago during the Ford administration, however, has prevented government from carrying out this mandate in the

new communication media such as cable TV, and in the 1990s even most public radio stations were privatized. Of course the government can err in regulating communication media. The important point, however, is that the market by its very nature excludes rational deliberation upon the public good. Whereas democratic government gives us the opportunity to collectively decide what the public good is and how the communication media will serve it, and perhaps make mistakes in doing so, the market precludes the possibility of there being any public good, and therefore will certainly fail to deliver it.

Chief among the public goods that the unregulated information market fails to deliver is civic education. It is unreasonable to expect any private business to foster critical thinking and responsible citizenship, two essential components of a civic education—not because business leaders necessarily have any conscious plan to keep us all gullible and politically passive, but because it is in the nature of any business to view its clients as consumers, not citizens or critics, and therefore to promote the values and habits of consumption, which as we have seen are not those of education. Information produced for consumers most often comes in the form of entertainment. It panders to consumers rather than educating or edifying them. Its purpose is pleasure for consumers and profit for the owners of the means of producing it. Consumers are encouraged to buy on impulse, not to reflect upon or improve their desires. That is why our best opportunity to effectively challenge our desires and improve them comes not in the act of consumption but in rational deliberation with fellow citizens.

Recall that in Plato's dialogues Socrates is brought to trial by corrupt politicians on false charges. Corrupt politicians, Socrates tells us, "gratify their hearers, sacrificing the public interest to their own personal success, and treating

their audience like children, whom their only object is to
please . . . but true virtue consists in fulfilling those desires
whose satisfaction makes a man better and denying those
which make him worse." (Plato, 1960: 110) Socrates knows
that he cannot win against those who pander to the crowd.

> So because what I say on any occasion is not designed to
> please, and because I aim not at what is most agreeable but
> at what is best, and will not employ the subtle arts which
> you advise, I shall have no defence to offer in a court of
> law. I can only repeat what I was saying to Polus; I shall be
> like a doctor brought before a tribunal of children at the
> suit of a confectioner. Imagine what sort of defence a man
> like that could make before such a court if he were accused
> in the following terms: 'Children, the accused has commit-
> ted a number of crimes against you; he is the ruin of even
> the youngest among you with his surgery and cautery; he
> reduces you to a state of helpless misery by choking you
> with bitter draughts and inflicting upon you a regime of
> starvation which cuts you off from food and drink. What a
> contrast to the abundant and varied luxury with which I
> have entertained you.' What do you think that the doctor
> could find to say in such a plight? If he were to utter the
> truth and tell the children that he had done all these things
> in the interest of their health, think of the prodigious outcry
> that a court so constituted would raise. (Plato, 1960: 140)

Corrupt politicians are like confectioners and entertainers.
They produce words or images which give us immediate
pleasure but have no lasting beneficial effect. True statesmen on the other hand are like doctors of medicine and
educators. They produce words or images which may not
be immediately pleasant to receive but which edify or serve
the real good of their audience. Now, only reason enables
us to distinguish between immediate pleasures and the real
good. Socrates cannot hope to persuade the jury because

they are like children who have not yet learned to reason. In this respect consumers are like unschooled children. They too are unlikely to choose the real good over immediate pleasure. They too respond well to those who pander to them and poorly to those who attempt to educate them. This is why Benjamin Barber (1995: 116-117) believes that education cannot compete with entertainment in the marketplace. Education is hard work. Though it promises a higher good for ourselves and our communities, education offers few of the immediate rewards that consumers expect. While entertainment flatters us with fantasies that make us feel better about ourselves, education challenges us to grow into our better selves. While consumer markets encourage us to act impulsively and greedily in isolation from one another, education disciplines our beliefs and desires through shared conversation and criticism. In order to engage in rational deliberation upon the common good, then, we must get out of our roles as consumers. And that requires a public space beyond the marketplace.

The postmodern information economy inverts the traditional hierarchical relationship between words and images, reason and the appetites, right and might, mind and body. In Plato's allegory of the divided line, the upper part of the line consists of invisible things that can be known only by the mind, or by thought. These include moral principles and mathematical concepts. The lower part of the line consists of those things that can be perceived by the body's senses. These include external objects perceived by the body's senses as well as internal bodily sensations and bodily desires or "appetites." The upper and lower parts of the line can themselves be divided into upper and lower parts, in the same proportion as the first division of the line into upper and lower parts. The upper part of the visible consists of visible spatio-temporal objects, such as sunflowers. The lower part of the visible consists of shadows or reflections of spatio-temporal objects. The upper part of the invisible consists of moral ideas, aspects of the good, such as justice, courage, wisdom and temperance. These are known by means of dialectical reasoning. The lower part of the invisible consists of mathematical, musical and astronomical truths—all of which for the Greeks were essentially one. These are known by means of deductive reasoning.

According to Plato each upper part is related to each lower part in an analogous fashion. The lower part is always an inferior shadow of the upper part. And the lower part is always many relative to the unity of the upper part. For example, a sunflower casts many shadows, but there is only one sunflower. There are many sets of three objects in the spatio-temporal domain, but there is only one number three. At the apex of Plato's system the Good is Unity itself. Justice is an aspect of the Good that makes it possible for people to cooperate with one another and avoid conflict. Wisdom is an aspect of the Good that makes it possible for a community to share a common truth and achieve consensus. Aspects of the Good are known by means of moral reasoning embodied in rational human speech *(logos)*. Without moral reasoning a community is doomed to suffer perpetual strife and conflict.

In Plato's allegory of the cave, puppets manipulated in front of a fire project shadows onto the wall of the cave. Prisoners in the cave are restrained in such a way that they can only see the shadows, but not the puppets or the fire behind them. A tunnel leads out of the cave into broad daylight, where objects such as sunflowers follow the course of the sun across the sky. The cave corresponds to the lower part of the divided line. It consists of spatio-temporal objects (the puppets) and their shadows. We perceive objects there with our senses and desire those objects that give us pleasure. The world outside the cave corresponds to the upper part of the divided line. It consists of the good itself (the sun), moral ideas or forms (the sunflower), and their shadows (the mathematical forms). We know objects outside the cave by way of the *logos,* the moral order of the cosmos reflected in rational human speech. In the cave allegory we see that the lower part of each divided line is not only an inferior shadow of the upper part, but that the lower part is an illusion relative to the greater truth of the upper part. So long as the prisoners see only the shadows but not the puppets themselves, they mistake the shadows for things themselves, the many for the One. Liberation from the cave is release into the enlightened world above.

The postmodern information economy subordinates words to images that are produced for pleasure and profit. Images whet our appetites and generate emotions such as greed, lust, fear and envy more effectively than words, while short circuiting moral reasoning. The result is a culture that uncannily resembles Plato's cave. The shadows in Plato's cave are images projected onto pixilated screens. The puppeteers are the handful of media conglomerates. In the postmodern information economy, says Benjamin Barber (1995: 127-128), reality has been replaced by virtuality, and consumers have become prisoners in Plato's cave. Words and conversation have been replaced by the passive consumption of images. But without words and the ideas they carry *(logos),* moral reasoning becomes impossible, and we cannot achieve justice, cooperation, or a common life together (a rational public sphere). Commerce proceeds apace, however, since images prove to be excellent devices for generating consumer needs, or, as Plato calls them, "appetites."

Of course, when Barber uses the term 'democracy' he is referring to deliberative democracy, a form of democracy in which citizens reason with one another about the common good, not to the consumer model of electoral democracy which exists in the United States today. In the consumer model, advertisers sell political candidates to the public with images designed to provoke emotion and short circuit reason. There is little or no rational public debate. The most entertaining candidates win and sometimes the winning candidates are entertainers. The consumer model of electoral democracy resembles what Plato refers to as simply as "democracy," a system ruled not by reason but by appetite. Whereas Plato believed that only the few could ever learn to reason on matters of public concern, and therefore participate in a deliberative democracy, Barber clings to the hope born of the Enlightenment that the rational public sphere can be expanded to include ever wider circles of the population.

Even when markets function according to their ideal, they fail to sustain democracy because they promote neither reason nor the public good. But as Soros points out, markets, like any other historical idea, have a way of self-destructing just when they are most successful. In the case of the market, the dialectical dynamic causes the competitive free market to devolve into the monopoly capitalism of a few major players, regulated by an overweening centralized state. Since the 1970s the government part of the equation has come under attack while the business side has enjoyed increasing power and prestige. While Vietnam and Watergate contributed to the public's disenchantment with government, the slump in profits motivated business leaders to roll back the populist gains of the 1930s and 1960s. By the 1990s, as Thomas Frank tells the story, the working class had been vanquished, but in the absence of the older populism, a new ideology was needed to legitimate the newly deregulated monopoly capitalist system. The ideology that evolved among pro-business opinion leaders was that of market populism, an ideology which equates the market with democracy. But market populism takes as its model the ideal of a perfectly competitive and efficient market. So upon critical scrutiny market populism fails in two respects: it fails because even ideal markets fail to promote reason or the public good, and therefore democracy, and it fails because the economic reality of our times is that of deregulated monopoly capitalism, not ideal markets.

Plato believed that any society contains the seeds of its own destruction. And that is certainly true of postmodern consumer capitalism. The emergence of religious fundamentalism since the 1970s is, in dialectical fashion, at one and the same time a reaction against the death of God and an outgrowth of the irrationalism already present within postmodern consumer capitalism. However, while the attacks on the World Trade Towers make for spectacular film footage, an even more potent threat to postmodern society than fundamentalism is the ensuing chaos of a society bereft of moral reasons or rules—a state of society anticipated by Plato who predicted that market democracy inevitably devolves into anarchy before devolving further into tyranny and madness.

11. Markets, Bureaucracies and New Economy Management Theory

Already near the end of the nineteenth century markets in the industrially developed nations had devolved into a monopoly capitalist system. Labor immediately responded by organizing against big business, while the regulatory state was created slightly later during the Progressive era. A system developed in which the anti-democratic nature of big business was accepted only because it was balanced by the democratic forces of labor and government. Throughout most of the twentieth century the power of organized labor and the regulatory state continued to grow until finally the shortage of capital in the 1970s prompted business leaders to radically reevaluate their strategies. Samuel P. Huntington, writing in a Trilateral Commission Report in 1975, argued that social instability was due to an excess of democracy, while Daniel Bell (1976) believed that the traditional Protestant work ethic was threatened by excessive affluence. The implication of these arguments was that in order to save liberal capitalism it was necessary to reduce the economic and political power of the American working class. Thus the social contract of the early postwar years, according to which the American working class would acquiesce in the imperialist adventures of the ruling class in return for a middle class lifestyle, was broken. The domestic working class would be brought down to the level of foreign workers through free trade agreements and open door immigration policies. Business investment would be directed to developing nations in Latin America and Asia. For example, in the 1970s the Treasury Department pressured US banks to recycle Arab petrodollars into developing nations in order to maintain the international trade system (Kapstein, 1994).

By the 1990s business had succeeded in rolling back organized labor and the regulatory state to such an extent that it had created a new crisis of legitimacy. Whereas during the 1970s business felt threatened by an excess of democracy, by the 1990s growing economic inequality caused business leaders to feel threatened by the appearance of insufficient democracy. The solution worked out by business propagandists in the 1990s was not to restore organized labor and the regulatory state, but to reject the former presumption that business and the marketplace are opposed to democracy and present them instead as the true guardians of democracy. According to market populism the market is an inherently democratic system. By applying the laws of the market to the inner workings of the corporation it too would appear to become a democratic institution. Whereas traditional corporate management techniques were highly bureaucratic, such that the internal organization of the corporation resembled nothing so much as the centralized command and control economies of the former Soviet bloc nations, the New Economy management techniques of the 1990s sought to emulate the workings of the market, bringing democracy to American corporations just as the fall of the Berlin wall was supposed to bring democracy to the former Soviet bloc nations.

The modern world has witnessed two interrelated but distinct trends. On the one hand, the market has expanded, but on the other hand, power has become concentrated in an increasingly large, centralized state, and in ever fewer large corporations, whose internal organization is not that of a market, but of a bureaucracy. Although the development of bureaucracy in the modern world appears to contradict the expansion of markets, markets actually depend upon bureaucratic forms of organization. Markets depend upon the rule of law imposed by the bureaucratic state. And markets concentrate economic power in the hands of a few large corporate bureaucracies because bureaucracies have proven to be more efficient and productive than other forms of organization. But a bureaucracy is not a market. It is a hierarchical system of command and control based upon formally defined rules of operation. Bureaucracies first appeared in the modern world as alternatives to feudal power. Recall that power in the feudal world is based upon highly personal ties of fealty between lord and vassal. There is relatively little notion of an abstract or formal system of law that all persons must obey regardless of who they are. Early modern absolutist states in eighteenth century France and Prussia were the first institutions to replace personal, feudal relationships with bureaucratic structures of organization. According to the Prussian German sociologist Max Weber all modern societies tend to replace forms of organization based upon personal relationships with bureaucracies based upon formally defined rules of operation. Of course, modern institutions may be corrupted by personal favoritism, nepotism, or personal loyalties. But when they do so they sacrifice efficiency and are punished by failing to meet their goals in the marketplace or in the political arena. Thus, according to Weber, bureaucratic rules and procedures are based upon rational considerations of efficiency and productivity. The most important reason that bureaucracies have been successful in the modern world is that they are technically superior to other forms of organization in just the same way as mechanical production is superior to non-mechanical production.

Weber defines power as the ability to achieve desired ends, despite resistance from others. Authority is power accepted as legitimate by those subjected to it. Weber said authority may be divided into three basic forms: charismatic, traditional, and rational-legal. Rationality may be divided into moral and technical reason. Whereas moral rationality is concerned with ends, technical rationality is concerned only with the means for achieving ends we have already chosen. The Prussian German philosopher Immanuel Kant's categorical imperative—according to which one must act in accordance with those moral rules that could be adopted by all rational agents—is the purest statement of moral reason. Technical rationality, on the other hand, is hypothetical. It tells us what we must do *if* we wish to achieve certain ends in the most efficient manner possible. It does not tell us what we must do in an absolute sense, but only what me must do relative to our chosen ends. In the early modern absolutist states the monarch chose the ends while the bureaucracy sought out efficient means to achieve them. A bureaucracy is a form of power that is legitimated by technical rational-legal authority. Its legitimacy rests on the fact that it is the most efficient means of achieving chosen ends, not on the fact that those ends are necessarily right.

According to Weber's ideal type of bureaucracy the most efficient form of organization includes these features: hierarchical chain of command and supervision, impartiality, comprehensive written rules and procedures, impersonality, appointment to office based on technical competency, specialized division of labor, and training for specific job titles. Power resides in the office not the person. Offices are occupied by qualified personnel but cannot be owned. Rules are objectively defined and applied impartially to all members of the organization. Appointments are made on the basis of objective qualifications rather than ascribed status or personal favors.

In 1911 the American engineer Frederick W. Taylor published *The Principles of Scientific Management*. Taylor's theory of efficient organization includes all the features of Weber's ideal bureaucracy and adds further refinements. According to Taylor's theory of scientific management the most efficient form of organization is based on the scientific analysis of work, scientifically designed procedures, the scientific selection, training, and development of workers, and the division of labor between workers and managers. One of the features of Taylor's theory of scientific management that workers objected to is that instead of allowing workers to design their own methods, expert managers designed them and workers had only to implement them. Taylor did not want unions in the workplace either, because he did not want them to interfere with his scientific design of work routines. In his defense Taylor argued that even managers in his system were governed by rules and laws which scientific experiments were supposed to have shown will maximize efficiency and that both workers and managers would be rewarded with higher wages and income in proportion to their rising productivity. Another complaint about Taylor's system was that it reduced workers to machines, since the work process was engineered in precisely the same way that a machine would be, in accordance with the laws of Newtonian mechanics. Taylor analyzed workers movements in fine detail and eliminated unnecessary movements in order to increase the speed of production. In this respect Taylor belonged to a long tradition of social engineering going back to the Enlightenment whose conception of reason was derived from Newtonian mechanics. The ultimate expression of a theory of knowledge derived from physics came in the early twentieth century, at the same time that Taylor's theories were popular, with the logical positivists, who claimed that empirical science is the only source of knowledge and that therefore there can be no knowledge of the human mind or of values.

The Weber-Taylor bureaucracy became the paradigm for efficient organizations throughout the industrialized world in the early twentieth century. In the United States Taylorism was adopted by the Ford Motor Company, B. F. Goodrich and many other large corporations that fueled the consumer economy. Although Taylorism came under increasing criticism from management experts by the beginning of the Second World War, it reached its zenith in the 1950s and remained the reigning paradigm for large organizations all the way up until the fall of the Berlin wall in 1989.

The Weber-Taylor bureaucracy was especially well represented in Germany where monopoly capitalism was somewhat less restricted than in the United States and Great Britain. Germany in the late nineteenth century had not fully emerged from feudalism. Whereas Great Britain and the United States passed through a period of small scale liberal markets before devolving into monopoly capitalism, Germany passed directly from feudalism, where free markets did not exist, to monopoly capitalism ruled by the Junker aristocracy, where free markets did not exist either. Consequently German corporations grew to very large proportions and, under the influence of Prussian models of administration, they adopted the Weber-Taylor bureaucratic form of organization.

In the United States Henry Ford and John D. Rockefeller admired German models of administration and established important alliances with German businesses. In Russia the German model found an admirer in the figure of Vladimir Lenin: "Here (in Germany) we have the 'last word' in modern large-scale engineering and planned organization, *subordinated to Junker-bourgeois imperialism.* Cross out the words in italics, and in place of the militarist, Junker, bourgeois, imperialist *state* put *also a state,* but of a different class content—a *Soviet* state, that is, a proletarian state, and you will have the *sum total* of the conditions necessary for socialism." (quoted in Taber, 1988: 44 from "'Left-Wing' Childishness and the Petty Bourgeois Mentality," *Collected Works,* Vol. 27, p. 334) Lenin was especially impressed by the German postal system. "A witty German Social-Democrat of the seventies of the last century called the *postal service* an example of the socialist economic system. This is very true. . . . To organize the *whole* economy on the lines of the postal service. . . all under the control and leadership of the armed proletariat—this is our immediate aim. This is the state and this is the economic foundation we need." (quoted in Taber, 1988: 60 from *The State and Revolution,* in *Collected Works,* Vol. 25, pp. 426-7)

Lenin admired the German bureaucracies because he believed as Max Weber did that the Weber-Taylor bureaucracy is technically superior to other forms of organization in just the same way as mechanical production is superior to non-mechanical production. Lenin believed that Russia's most pressing problem was poverty and underdevelopment and that therefore its most urgent need was to undergo rapid industrialization. In order to achieve that aim it was necessary not only to import German technology but also German techniques of industrial management. Since the Weber-Taylor bureaucracy was viewed in purely technical terms, Lenin believed that it would be possible to retain the technical advantages of the Weber-Taylor bureaucracy while subordinating it to different ends, in this case, to the interests of the working class rather than the bourgeoisie.

> Although they were fiercely opposed to tradi-
> tional capitalism, capitalist corporations and banks
> and individual capitalists, the Bolsheviks were ex-
> tremely fond of bourgeois technology, particularly
> the techniques of capitalist industry.
> But their attachment was not limited to merely
> the industrial processes, as such—technology in the
> narrow sense of the term—but to the overall meth-
> ods and even structure of capitalist industry. This
> included the centralization, the hierarchical struc-
> ture of management, piecework and other facets of
> (bourgeois) "scientific management" (e.g., Tay-
> lorism).
> Lenin actually believed that the overall struc-
> ture and methods of capitalist industry could be
> taken over, in toto, by a proletarian state. (Taber,
> 1988: 44)

But there is a problem. A socialist economy is not
merely one that serves the interests of the working class. It
is one that is directly controlled by the workers. But the
Weber-Taylor bureaucracy is not a democratic system. It is
a highly centralized and hierarchical organization. It provides no mechanism for the workers themselves to control
the productive process. Indeed the workers are treated as
cogs in the industrial machine. Although Lenin spoke of
organizing the economy under the control and leadership
of the armed proletariat, he also believed that the centrali-
zation of power in a single will was necessary for more efficient production. "Lenin's commitment to, virtual adora-
tion of, centralism can be seen in his fairly frequent rec-
ommendation that the economy, revolutionary army, and
soviet state be 'subordinated to a single will' (presumably
his)." (Taber, 1988: 41) Thus when Lenin spoke of organizing the economy under the control and leadership of the

armed proletariat, what he really meant was that the economy would be organized under his will in the interest of the working class. Only a highly centralized and hierarchical system such as the Weber-Taylor bureaucracy could, in Lenin's opinion, achieve the levels of production necessary to raise the condition of the working class in Russia. "The organization of accounting, the control of large enterprises, the transformation of the state economic mechanism into a single huge machine, into an economic organism that will work in such a way as to enable hundreds of millions of people to be guided by a single plan—such was the enormous organizational problem that rested on our shoulders." (Lenin, quoted in Taber, 1988: 41 from the Political Report of the Central Committee to the Extraordinary Seventh Congress of the RCP(B), delivered March 7, 1918. *Collected Works,* Vol. 27, pp. 90-91.) The net result was that the Soviet Union became a state capitalist society organized along the lines of a Weber-Taylor bureaucracy—but not a socialist society.

Lenin sought to do for Russia what the Ford Motor Company did for the United States: utilize the techniques of mechanical production and Weber-Taylor management to increase production of a uniform product on a massive scale. Thanks to an even more successful application of these techniques than Ford was able to implement, the Soviet Union underwent an extremely rapid process of industrialization. But beginning in the 1950s the Weber-Taylor paradigm began to unravel in the United States. Markets became saturated with uniform products designed to satisfy the "lowest common denominator." To increase production further it was necessary to divide or segment the market into smaller parts. Instead of producing uniform products for the greatest number of undifferentiated consumers, the American economy increasingly produced different products for limited segments of the population which were distinguished by their unique consumer desires. Market segmentation allowed the American economy to continue growing while the Soviet economy never progressed beyond the level reached by the United States in the 1950s. The Soviet Union successfully mastered the techniques of production. But it failed to manage consumption in the way the infotainment telesector would come to do in the United States. While the American economy developed into postmodern consumer capitalism, the Soviet Union remained at the stage of industrial capitalism.

In spite of every effort to achieve critical distance from their opposition, leftist movements are always colored by their age. Lenin wished to break from industrial capitalism but retained its techniques of production and management. While industrial capitalism produced for uniform mass markets, the left sought to organize the working class into a unified mass bound together by solidarity. As industrial capitalism transformed into consumer capitalism, and as markets became segmented, the left divided the working class into special interest groups defined by their unique identities. By the 1960s consumerism and market segmentation had begun to alter the techniques of production. The Old Left in the United States disliked the Weber-Taylor bureaucracy because it alienated workers from their labor. But by the 1960s the New Left disliked Taylorism because it induced conformity and inhibited spontaneous individual expression. Taylorism was "square." While the Old Left disliked Taylorism because it robbed workers of their work (production), the New Left disliked Taylorism because it robbed workers of their play (consumption). Thus in the 1990s when the New Economy management theorists began their assault on the Weber-Taylor bureaucracy in favor of market oriented techniques of management, they were able to successfully co-opt the language of the New Left liberation movements.

Although capitalist markets were largely responsible for the creation of the Weber-Taylor bureaucracy, it presented those markets with at least two major problems. First, the success of the Weber-Taylor bureaucracy in managing production raised the possibility that the entire economy could be scientifically managed, as Lenin attempted to do in Russia, and that the market could therefore be eliminated. Second, markets have always sought legitimacy as mediums of consent and exchange between parties who stand on an equal footing with one another. But the Weber-Taylor bureaucracy is a hierarchical, top-down command and control system. Workers must obey the commands given to them or seek employment in another bureaucracy where they will also be issued commands. In the case of bureaucracies which hold a monopoly or near monopoly in their industry, workers don't even have that option.

In the 1920s the AT & T corporation sought to defuse public outrage over its coercive power in the workplace and a series of bloody battles with unions in the preceding decade by instituting employee representation schemes. The Human Relations school of management theory founded by Elton Mayo at AT & T in the 1920s was the first major challenge to Taylorism. It too arose directly out of AT & T's need to preempt union organizing efforts and appear more democratic. Then in the 1950s and 1960s as consumerism took off there was a rising tide of sentiment within the corporate world against the Weber-Taylor bureaucracy. Books like William H. Whyte's *Organization Man* expressed the fear that the nation was being turned into an army of conformists dressed in identical gray flannel suits. Corporate strategists worried that the Weber-Taylor bureaucracy inhibited innovation and consumption. They needed workers who could think "outside the box" and consumers who were motivated to chase the latest fashions. Following a decade of deregulation and union busting the corporate world faced a similar crisis of legitimacy in the 1990s, and it responded in the same way it had in the 1920s: by replacing Taylorism with the methods and buzzwords of a new, more "democratic" school of management. But the "democracy" that New Economy management theory brings to corporate management is not the democracy we associate with voting or public deliberation. It is the democracy of market populism, the democracy of the market. By "marketizing" the corporation, New Economy management gurus claimed to "liberate" us, and in doing so they used all the same rhetoric the Left had used generations before. They presented their struggle against scientific management as a class struggle that would promote democracy and liberate the oppressed from the yoke of economic injustice (Frank, 2000: 186).

In his 1992 book *Liberation Management* Tom Peters "named the new categorical imperative that was freeing everybody: *'blasting the violent winds of the marketplace into every nook and cranny in the firm.'*" (Frank, 2000: 189). The idea of the market was the organizing principle behind most of the big management ideas of the 1990s. "The corporation 'delayered,' throwing off entire levels of management; it 'disaggregated,' ridding itself of its extraneous operations; it embraced 'flexibility,' making it easier to replace career employees with (zero-benefits) temps; it 'outsourced' every possible piece of work to the lowest bidder; it 'reengineered' its various processes in a less labor-intensive way; it 'disintermediated,' using new technology to cut out middlemen and move back office jobs to wherever wages were lowest." (Frank, 2000: 191) The logical culmination of this idea would be for the permanent staff of the corporation to be reduced to the upper level managers who make the deals. All other employees would be "marketized." They would be hired as needed on a temporary basis without benefits or union representation. The genius of market populism was to sell these new management techniques to the public as a form of liberation.

This was done in part by portraying the old corporate system as a totalitarian system comparable to the Soviet Union (Frank, 2000: 211). As we have seen there is a legitimate basis to this comparison. The structure of both the state managed economy in the Soviet Union and the American blue-chip corporation of the 1950s could be traced back to the centralized, bureaucratic structure of the Prussian state. But New Economy management theorists were not proposing to hand over the management of American corporations to workers. Instead, they proposed to liberate American workers by "marketizing" the corporation.

The basic idea of the New Economy was that changes in information technology had changed the way that the economy operates. Since technological change was viewed as an act of nature beyond human control these changes in the way the economy operates were viewed as inevitable. Luckily for investors the new economic laws justified the high price of internet stocks. They also made government regulation of the market impossible. Market populism gave the deregulated market moral legitimacy by equating the market with democracy. Wriston was the CEO of Citibank. His book *The Twilight of Sovereignty* was the seminal text of New Economy thought. Wriston argued that information technology had brought about changes to the way business operates that were as significant and dramatic as the Industrial Revolution. Consequently all attempts to regulate business were obsolete. For example, Wriston argued that the internet had made it impossible to regulate global currency markets. But this was not to be regretted because the global currency markets are "global plebiscites" that pass democratic judgement on a government's policies. Walter Wriston was particularly interested in repealing laws such as the Glass Steagall Act that prevented Citibank from merging with investment houses. The Glass-Steagall Act was passed after the Great Crash of 1929. Collusion between banks and investment houses had contributed to the stock market boom and subsequent crash in the 1920s. The Federal Government stepped in and pried the two industries apart. For generations bankers had wanted to repeal the Glass-Steagall Act and finally the Clinton Administration granted them their wish. In 1998 Citibank merged with the Travelers Insurance Group and Salomon Smith Barney, making it the largest financial services corporation in the world. Shortly thereafter Robert Rubin, Secretary of the Treasury under the Clinton Administration, became a highly paid executive at Citigroup. After the internet stock market bubble burst in 2000 Citigroup came under fire for improper collusion between the investment banking and brokerage arms of the firm. The Federal Government enacted new regulations and the SEC strengthened its enforcement procedures, but CEO Sandy Weill deflected most of the blame away from himself and breaking up Citigroup was never considered.

Those who defended the concept of the New Economy argued that changes in information technology made government or indeed any centralized regulation of markets impossible. If we were to think of "democracy" literally as collective "rule" *(kratein)* by the "people" *(demos),* we would not follow the next step in the argument, because the advocates of the concept of the New Economy argue that democracy will flourish once markets are deregulated. But to advocates of the concept of the New Economy, democracy is not a system of collective rule. Democracy is a free market in which individuals act without any constraints from centralized bodies. Thus, removing centralized control of an economic system should automatically create a democratic system. In his book *The Twilight of Sovereignty* Walter Wriston "recites how the VCR brought down Marcos, how the cassette tape brought down the Shah, and how TV destroyed Communism." (Frank, 2000: 55) Wriston suggests that by removing centralized control of the economy the new information technologies would bring down tyrants and allow democracy to flourish. But even if the new information technologies make certain kinds of tyranny more difficult to maintain, they do not necessarily promote democracy, as we have seen in the examples Wriston himself offers.

The internet was the most important technological development of the New Economy era and the one that was believed to hold the most radical implications for the political and economic system. What makes the internet different from television and radio is that information is sent and received from countless points in a network rather than being sent from a few centralized points to millions of viewers or listeners. The internet is more akin to the telephone, except that it allows for the efficient transmission of text and graphics as well as sound. Although the telephone network never prevented AT & T from achieving monopoly control over the telephone industry, fans of the New Economy argued that the decentralized nature of communication over the internet would bring down all centralized hierarchies and replace them with free markets. "For this vision of the internet as laissez-faire incarnate we have George Gilder to thank . . ." (Frank, 2000: 79) George

Gilder, a conservative columnist for *Forbes* magazine, believed that the internet spelled the end of hierarchies everywhere: "Rather than pushing decisions up through the hierarchy, the power of microelectronics pulls them remorsely down to the individual." (Gilder, quoted in Frank, 2000: 81) Other New Economy thinkers expanded the logic of the market to include the entire universe. Kevin Kelly discovered the principle of "distributed intelligence" in everything from the free market to robot design to living organisms of all kinds (Frank, 2000: 57). Attempts by government to regulate markets were therefore violations of a law of nature.

Kelly recommended outsourcing as the way to "revolutionize" corporations and replace vertical integration with distributed networks or markets. But what really irked the internet revolutionaries was the power of government and unions. In a December 1999 op-ed Thomas Friedman of the *New York Times* "compared the destruction of the Berlin Wall to the 'Internet revolution' on the grounds that the latter was stripping power (power to regulate 'capital flow,' that is) from 'governments and unions'." (Frank, 2000: 64) Meanwhile, Kevin Kelly hoped that encryption technology would stymie government attempts to regulate the market (Frank, 2000: 57).

Since the market is viewed as an act of nature rather than a product of human artifice, and since acts of nature are beyond human control, changes caused by the market are inevitable, and it is futile to resist them. For example, only a fool would resist global free trade policies, since they are based in the logic of the market. When protests broke out in Seattle in 1999 against the World Trade Organization and its free trade policies, New Economy pundits were quick to scold the protesters for attempting to stop the inevitable and accused them of having racist motives for wishing to block the growth of democracy (i.e., the market) in developing nations. Since market events are unintended acts of nature, changes caused by them cannot even be predicted or understood. New Economy management gurus preach intellectual humility in the face of the market. That's why corporate managers roll out the concept of change whenever they want to implement a new policy without any rational explanation. Accept the new policy, managers say like Buddhist holy men, because change is a mysterious but inevitable fact of life. In the past the concept of progress was used whenever business or government wished to ram through changes that the people resisted. But the concept of "change" is fundamentally different (Frank, 2000: 240).

When Robert Moses leveled city blocks to make way for modern housing projects in New York City, he did not deny responsibility for his action by claiming that it was an inevitable act of nature. Instead he appealed to the ideal of progress. Robert Moses claimed that the destruction of the old tenements was part of a rational engineering plan that was intended to improve living conditions in the city and serve the common good. But managers who use the concept of change to justify their policies make no pretense of implementing a rational plan, of improving society, or of serving the common good. Managers use the concept of change simply to evade responsibility for their actions, while the related concept of "inevitability" is a rhetorical device they use to push through changes that their workers don't want.

Bestsellers are often written at such a low level that the author of one bestseller admitted in his title that all he had learned he had learned in kindergarten. Spencer Johnson's *Who Moved My Cheese?* is no exception. Written as a parable about life in the corporate world, Spencer tells the story of mice who search for cheese after it has been moved. The moral of the story is supposed to be that one should not question change but merely accept it and move on. Spencer never does tell his readers who moved the cheese. That is supposed to be irrelevant since change is taken as a given to which we must adapt. But we know who moved the cheese: the corporate managerial class. It is in the interest of the corporate movers and shakers for the mice not to question why change occurs. But of course the managers know why change occurs. They know that change is not "inevitable." They know that change is not something that one must "adapt" to, because they are the ones who make the changes. Thus the real crime in questioning change is to infringe upon management's prerogative to formulate policy. The real crime is to cross the class boundary between those who are acted upon and those who act.

Most importantly what gets lost in this New Age cult of the market is the rule of law and reason. By preaching intellectual humility before the market, the New Economy management gurus prohibit any attempt to understand it in rational terms. Market events are to be viewed as unintended acts of nature to which we must adapt. Changes strike us like lightning bolts out of the blue. What appears to be anarchy and chaos to the mice, however, is really tyranny, because the absence of rational law in the workplace leaves managers free to rule by act of will. This suits our CEOs with their inflated egos and correspondingly high salaries perfectly well. But Plato would have called them mad. In a very real sense we have returned to the feudal ages when power was private, the public realm had fallen into decay, and barbarism had vanquished civilization based upon the rule of law.

12. Postmodern Consumer Capitalism and the Public Library

The dominant trend of the past half century has been the emergence of postmodern consumer capitalism. Public libraries are no exception to this trend. Indeed since the public library's original mission was to sustain a rational public sphere of discourse, its decline into a consumer information service offers a particularly clear if not magnified example of the emergence of postmodern consumer capitalism. Both the library's relationship to its clients and its internal organization have changed.

Whereas before, clients were expected to adhere to the bureaucratic rules and procedures of the library, today they are increasingly viewed as customers in a marketplace. Features of a bureaucracy include impartiality, comprehensive written rules and procedures, and impersonality. Rules are objectively defined and applied impartially to all members and clients of the organization. But in a market all terms of service are negotiable at the point of transaction. Thus, under a market model, if a customer owes the library a fine, he can negotiate with the library to reduce or eliminate his fine. In the interest of "good customer service" and preserving its relationship with the customer the library may agree to reduce the fines owed by some customers who aggressively negotiate lower fines, while others pay the standard fine. The library might even choose to overlook stolen material if on balance it gains by doing so. Indeed since public libraries receive funding from third parties there is little incentive to do otherwise. This same laissez-faire attitude applies to all the rules of the market-oriented public library.

The basic principle of New Economy management theory is to replace bureaucratic structures with market mechanisms, or as Tom Peters put it in his 1992 book *Liberation Management: "blasting the violent winds of the marketplace into every nook and cranny in the firm."* (quoted in Frank, 2000: 189) The market-oriented library prefers that its employees relate to one another as they would in the marketplace. Full time permanent employees are encouraged to view one another as "customers." But the market-oriented library hires relatively few permanent full time employees with benefits. It prefers to draw labor from the marketplace as needed on a temporary contractual basis. It does not value loyalty and discourages long term employment. It offers early retirement incentives to long term employees and then hires them back as temporary workers. It hires part time paraprofessionals or even opens its doors to poorly qualified volunteers.

Markets are flexible, dynamic processes. That's why the only thing that doesn't change, as we are constantly reminded, is change itself. During the New Economy era most changes were attributed to information technology. But machines don't manage change. People in positions of power do. Machines, even computers, do only what they are told to do. Most of the changes we experienced during the New Economy era were due to aggressive market-oriented management policies, not to technology alone. Technology merely gives management the tools to carry out its policies. For example, if automated book selection replaces librarians that will only be because management has decided that critical judgement is no longer needed in book selection.

The greatest reduction of in-house labor during the New Economy era was due to outsourcing, reengineered work routines, removing layers of management and supervision, and downsizing; not to automation. Most technological innovations such as web-based catalogs improved the quality of service but did little to reduce labor needs. Outsourcing allows an organization to replace an internal bureaucratic relationship to its employees with a market relationship to an outside vendor. Outsourcing to distant locations allows organizations to circumvent local government regulations and unions in search of cheap labor. In locations where labor is expensive such as the coastal cities of the Northeast or West Coast, back office jobs such as cataloging or book processing can be outsourced to companies in the Southeast or Midwest. Telephone and web-based reference services could someday be outsourced to India where there is a well educated English speaking population willing to work for lower wages and fewer benefits. But outsourcing can occur locally, too. For example, a library might hire an outside company to provide custodial services at lower cost.

New Economy management theory claims that by removing layers of supervision, and by replacing pyramidal chains of management with a distributed web-like decision making network, we will be liberated from bureaucratic structures. But instead of liberating us these new management techniques merely create a more dysfunctional bureaucracy. A bureaucratic system that pretends to be a distributed network, but is not, is the worst of all possible worlds. In their contempt for bureaucratic rules and procedures, market management techniques tend to neglect the system of rules and procedures which check the personal power of managers. Furthermore, contradictions arise when web-like network structures are imposed on bureaucratic systems. A "flattened hierarchy" is one in which layers of supervision have been removed. But it is still a hierarchy. It is simply one in which there is less adequate and fair supervision. Attempts to replace pyramidal chains of supervision with web-like networks of supervision lead to conflict and confusion. They can also be unjust. A bureaucracy is a top-down hierarchical chain of command and supervision. Typically the hierarchy is arranged in a pyramid. At the top of the pyramid a single individual manages and supervises a group of individuals at the immediate level below. Those individuals in turn each manage and supervise a group of individuals below them. Lines of command and supervision do not overlap or intersect with one another. Each member of the organization reports to one and only one immediate supervisor. If there is a conflict between an individual and that individual's supervisor that they cannot resolve themselves, the conflict must be resolved at a higher level by the supervisor's supervisor. However, in a bureaucratic system supervisory authority is based upon a rational system of rules and procedures known to everyone. A bureaucracy is based upon the rule of law, not personal will.

An ideal market is not a pyramidal hierarchy but a distributed network like the internet in which decisions are made independently at each node in the network. When a link is established in the network it occurs bilaterally with the consent of both nodes. If two nodes in the network cannot resolve their differences they simply discontinue their relationship and break the link between them. There is no central authority to resolve differences. Nor are there any universal rules except the basic principles of contract and reciprocal exchange.

Ideal markets don't exist. They are theoretical models that apply to real world events only within certain strict boundary conditions. They assume, for instance, that all links in the network are consensual and that no node possesses unilateral power over another. In the real world we are connected to others in ways we did not and could not choose, and some individuals possess power over others. Markets cannot substitute for democratic systems of governance which allow us to make collective decisions about matters of common interest and the ties that bind us together.

New Economy management attempts to impose market structures on bureaucratic systems are disingenuous. Imposing a web-like structure of supervision or flattening the hierarchy by removing layers of supervision does not a market make. Power differentials remain. Links are not consensual or bilateral, and workers have little opportunity to sever or reconstruct links within the organization at will as they would in a genuine free market. Nor do such strategies transform the bureaucracy into a democracy, since democracy requires rational deliberation in a public domain about matters of common interest. Even ideal markets fail to construct public spaces or to recognize common interests.

Librarian work routines have been reengineered by eliminating their role as gatekeepers of the culture. According to Twitchell (1992), between 1850 and 1950 high culture was separated off from popular culture by the presence of a gatekeeper who determined what would be admitted into high culture. At least until 1950, and perhaps as late as the introduction of the paperback book and the conglomeration of the entertainment industry in the 1970s and 1980s, the selection of printed texts was viewed as the most important function of the gatekeeper, because print was viewed as the foundation of the culture. In Umberto Eco's fable about a medieval monastery, librarians serve as the paradigmatic gatekeepers of the culture. Due to the influence of Melvil Dewey and the defining down of the profession, librarians in the United States always had an ambivalent relationship to their role as gatekeepers. But if librarians in the United States had been partly reduced to clerical intermediaries in the process of selecting printed texts, at least they were still positioned at the gate. In the era of the New Economy there was no gate to keep.

Public libraries in the United States were never the exclusive preserve of high culture. For example, public libraries housed large collections of popular novels throughout the twentieth century. But at least until 1950 popular books were provided to the public because it was hoped that once the public's appetite for them had been quenched they would turn to more elevating material. It was therefore essential that the librarian know the difference between high and low culture and be able to maintain a collection in both. Librarians in the nineteenth century were no different from other Victorians who worried about the rising tide of popular culture. Throughout the Colonial period and into the nineteenth century Americans founded libraries and literary societies and enjoyed a surprisingly high rate of literacy. But in the wake of rapid social changes many Victorians became concerned about a decline in reading standards. In the inaugural issue of the *American Library Journal* William Frederick Poole, who was the director of the Chicago Public Library, wrote that "there is in the mental development of every person who later attains to literary culture a limited period when he craves novel-reading; and perhaps reads novels to excess; but from which, if the desire be gratified, he passes safely out into broader fields of study, and this craving never returns to him in its original form." (quoted in Battles, 2003: 148) Poole's belief that it is the responsibility of the librarian to promote the intellectual growth and development of readers remained an important part of librarianship for much of the twentieth century. Librarians functioned as educators, and as such they needed to know something about their student-readers as well as the books they provided for them, so they could provide their student-readers with books that were at and above their stage of development. While librarians selected some books simply because their readers wanted them, they also selected books based on critical standards. Typically, librarians read critical reviews of books before selecting them. Librarians were well read and many reviews were written by librarians. Today the trend is moving away from selecting books on the basis of reviews or critical standards. Librarians' work routines have been reengineered to allow less time for reading. More and more books are selected only because they have high projected sales figures or they are in high demand. At the far end of this trend librarians no longer select books for their collections. At the far end of this trend we find automated book ordering systems that reorder titles based solely on their circulation or the number of requested holds, similar to the automated book ordering systems in corporate chain bookstores. To paraphrase Twitchell, shocking as it may seem to William Frederick Poole, the chief monk at the Chicago Public Library may soon be a technician looking at small blinking numbers on a computer screen. "Get me some more Danielle Steel and Stephen King," he says. Automated inventory systems are becoming the new gatekeepers, but what they admit into the library bears no resemblance to high culture. The principle of selection becomes quite simply, "give 'em what they want." Pander to your public's every wish; flatter them; patronize them; but don't try to educate them. The lack of critical standards attests to the nihilism at the heart of postmodern consumer culture.

As the role of the gatekeeper disappears from public libraries, popular culture overwhelms high culture, entertainment replaces education, and images replace print. Libraries now include large collections of videos as well as bestselling books written for movies. We are told that there is no difference between image and print because both contain information, and since the business of the library is to supply the public with information, we must provide both. But there is a difference between information and knowledge. Words are better able to convey abstract ideas and the knowledge they contain than images. Images may be more entertaining than words, but entertainment is merely the consumption of information for the purpose of obtaining pleasure, not knowledge. Insofar as the library becomes a purveyor of images it becomes part of the consumer economy.

The retail model is being applied to reference work as well. If you visit a Barnes & Noble's bookstore and ask a general reference question—say, "What is the population of China?"—they will either look at you with a blank stare or make an uninformed guess as to what kind of book would have the answer to your question. That's because Barnes & Noble's doesn't hire reference librarians. They hire poorly paid clerks who are trained to answer directional questions—in other words, to locate specific titles or subject areas on the shelves. If you ask a reader's advisory question—say, "Can you recommend a good work of historical fiction set in colonial New England?"—you will get a similar response. Retail clerks aren't expected to know anything about books or how to find information in them. They are there only to fetch books for you and to do it in a personable, friendly manner—service with a smile. Their job is really no different than waiting tables in a restaurant. They receive training in customer service, but not reference or reader's advisory service.

Chelton (2003) is right that the quality of reader's advisory services in most public libraries is poor, but she fails to explain why. The tenor of her article places the blame on librarians, and excludes their perspective. The reason reader's advisory service in most public libraries is poor is that like clerks in a corporate chain bookstore, librarians are receiving more training in customer service and less training in reference or reader's advisory service. Partly that's because that's what the public expects. "Customers" are much more likely to complain if they receive poor customer service from librarians than if they fail to get an answer to their reference or reader's advisory question. Indeed, customers ask far more directional questions than reference questions and ask even fewer reader's advisory questions. "Customers" have probably had more experience as shoppers than they have in libraries and tend to bring their expectations from their shopping experiences with them to the public library. Consequently, library administrators emphasize customer service over reference or reader's advisory service. Some have even hired marketing research firms to evaluate customer service in their libraries. One such firm, Service Evaluation Concepts, hires "mystery shoppers" to visit local establishments such as restaurants, hotels, gas stations, as well as libraries, as a consumer of goods and services, to evaluate customer service.

Once material selection, reference and reader's advisory are taken away from librarians, nothing remains of their traditional work duties but library management and customer service. Since these two remaining duties are different, and require different levels of education and training, they can be split into two separate roles.

Martin Gomez (2000), the director of the Brooklyn Public Library and candidate for president of the ALA during the New Economy era, proposed that the library profession establish an undergraduate degree program in library science to train paraprofessionals. This new class of library employee would have "increased responsibility for most of what we call 'traditional' librarian responsibilities." Another class of library employee with graduate degrees in library science "would no longer do collection development, cataloging or reference work but instead direct this work as performed by others with undergraduate degrees in library theory and practice. Librarians with MLS degrees would operate on a higher plane, developing and evaluating programs and institutional policies designed to meet community needs."

But since material selection, reference and reader's advisory are being phased out of the postmodern library of the 21st century, in practice Mr. Gomez's paraprofessionals would spend most of their day at the "information desk" delivering "customer service." Since they will not be performing many "traditional librarian responsibilities" it will surely occur to some future leader of the profession to dispense with undergraduate training in library science and hire any literate person they can find with adequate customer service experience. According to Mr. Gomez's vision librarians with graduate degrees will serve as managers of the library. But surely some future leader of the profession will see that individuals with degrees in business management or public planning are better qualified to be managers than librarians. This is the route by which librarians will be removed from libraries.

Bibliography

Archibold, Randal C. (2001), "What Kind of Education is Adequate? It Depends," in *The New York Times,* January 14, 2001, p. 33.

Ashby, Lou Anna (1977), "Library Company of Philadephia," in the *Journal of Library History,* vol. 12, no. 2 (Spring 1977).

Barber, Benjamin R. (1995), *Jihad vs. McWorld: How Globalism and Tribalism are Reshaping the World.* New York: Ballantine Books, 1995

Battles, Matthew (2003), *Library: An Unquiet History.* New York: W. W. Norton & Company, Inc.

Bell, Daniel (1976), *The Cultural Contradictions of Capitalism.* New York: Basic Books

Bellamy, Richard (1992), *Liberalism and Modern Society: A Historical Argument.* University Park, Pennsylvania: The Pennsylvania State University Press

Berman, Morris (2000), *The Twilight of American Culture.* New York: W. W. Norton & Company, Inc.

Bernstein, Richard (2003), "Pride in Austria on Schwarzenegger, but Less Joy Elsewhere," in *The New York Times,* posted online October 8, 2003.

Chelton, Mary (2003), "A crash course in RA: common mistakes librarians make and how to avoid them," in *Library Journal,* November 1, 2003

Cohen, Lizabeth (2003), *A Consumer's Republic: The Politics of Mass Consumption in Postwar America.* New York: Alfred A. Knopf

Ditzion, Sidney H. (1947), *Arsenals of a Democratic Culture: A Social History of the American Public Library Movement in New England and the Middle States from 1850-1900.* Chicago: American Library Association

Dodge, Chris (1998), "Taking Libraries to the Street: Infoshops & Alternative Reading Rooms," in *American Libraries,* May 1998.

Ezard, John (2003), "Buy Lattes and Get Online at Britain's First Idea Store: Library in Run-Down Area of East London Gets a Superstore-style makeover—and draws a new generation of readers," in *The Guardian,* February 15, 2003.

Frank, Thomas (2000), *One Market Under God: Extreme Capitalism, Market Populism, and the End of Economic Democracy.* New York: Doubleday

Gomez, Martin (2000), *Public Librarians for the 21st Century.* Downloaded 10/31/00 at www.ala.org/congress/gomez.html

Hanley, Robert (1998), "Jersey City Librarians Protest Plan for Private Contractor," in *The New York Times,* June 29, 1998, pp. B1 and B6.

Hayek, F. A. (1944), *The Road to Serfdom*. Chicago: The University of Chicago Press

Herbert, Bob (2003), "Bracing for the Blow," in *The New York Times*, December 26, 2003, p. A43.

Huntington, Samuel P. (1975), "The Democratic Distemper," in Michel Crozier, et al., editors, *The Crisis of Democracy*. New York: NYU Press

Johnson, Kirk (1996), "Searching for a Legacy of Libraries: Carnegie Descendant Finds Personal Stake in Historical Study," in *The New York Times*, November 28, 1996, pp. B1 and B8.

Jones, Theodore (1997), *Carnegie Libraries Across America: A Public Legacy*. New York: John Wiley & Sons, Inc.

Kapstein, Ethan B. (1994), *Governing the Global Economy: International Finance and the State*. Cambridge, Mass.: Harvard University Press

Kasson, John F. (1978), *Amusing the Million: Coney Island at the Turn of the Century*. New York: Hill & Wang

Lane, Megan (2003), "Is This the Library of the Future?" from BBC News Online, posted March 18, 2003.

McCook, Kathleen de la Pena (2001), "Poverty, Democracy and Public Libraries," in *Libraries & Democracy: The Cornerstones of Liberty*, pp. 28-46, edited by Nancy Kranich. American Library Association

Plato (1960), *Gorgias.* Translated by Walter Hamilton. New York, New York: Penguin Books

Plato (1985), *Republic.* Translated by Richard W. Sterling and William C. Scott. New York, New York: W. W. Norton & Company

Poggi, Gianfranco (1978), *The Development of the Modern State: A Sociological Introduction.* Stanford, California: Stanford University Press

Randall, John Herman (1940), *The Making of the Modern Mind: A Survey of the Intellectual Background of the Present Age.* Cambridge, Massachusetts: The Riverside Press

Rashbaum, William K. (2001), "Broad Plan Aims to Improve Police Rapport With Public," in *The New York Times,* January 15, 2001, p. 1

Reich, Wilhelm (1970), *The Mass Psychology of Fascism.* New York: Farrar, Strauss and Giroux

Rikowski, Ruth (2003), "Library Privatisation: Fact or Fiction?" in *Information for Social Change,* No. 17, Summer 2003. Available online at www.libr.org/ISC/

Sandel, Michael (1996), *Democracy's Discontent: America in Search of a Public Philosophy.* Cambridge, Massachusetts: Belknap Press of Harvard University Press

Shera, Jesse H. (1949), *Foundations of the Public Library: The Origins of the Public Library Movement in New England 1629-1855.* Reprint Edition (Hamden, CT: Shoestring Press, 1974)

Soros, George (1997), "The Capitalist Threat," in *The Atlantic Monthly*, February 1997, Volume 279, No. 2, pp. 45-58.

Stevenson, Richard W. (2002), "Government May Make Private Nearly Half of Its Civilian Jobs," in *The New York Times*, November 15, 2002, pp. A1 and A28.

Taber, Ron (1988), *A Look at Leninism.* New York: Aspect Foundation

Taylor, Frederick W. (1911), *The Principles of Scientific Management.* New York: Harper Brothers

Twitchell, James B. (1992), *Carnival Culture: The Trashing of Taste in America.* New York: Columbia University Press

Washburn, Katherine and Thornton, John (1996), editors of *Dumbing Down: Essays on the Strip-Mining of American Culture.* New York: W. W. Norton & Company

Zweizig, Douglas L. and Rodger, Eleanor Jo (1982), *Output Measures for Public Libraries: A Manual of Standardized Procedures.* Chicago: American Library Association

About the Author

Ed D'Angelo was born in Brooklyn, New York, where the schools, libraries and his own family taught him to value education and the cultural ferment of the 1960s instilled in him a passion for inquiry and intellectual discovery. Attending college in New York State with the aid of scholarships, teaching assistantships and fellowships just before the cost of education started to escalate, he earned six degrees in three fields, including a B.S. summa cum laude in Computer & Systems Engineering from Rensselaer Polytechnic Institute, a Ph.D. in Philosophy from the State University of New York at Stony Brook, and an M.L.S. from the State University of New York at Albany. In his dissertation at Stony Brook Dr. D'Angelo developed a theory of consciousness that drew upon the works of Carl Jung, Friedrich Nietzsche and modern neuroscience. Between 1988 and 1992 he served as an Adjunct Assistant Professor of Philosophy at Rensselaer Polytechnic Institute and at other colleges and universities in New York's Capital District. He taught the history of philosophy, the philosophy of religion and political philosophy. In 1992 he returned to Brooklyn to work at the Brooklyn Public Library. Between 1994 and 1998 he served on the collective that opened Blackout Bookstore and Infoshop in New York's Lower East Side. Today he is a Supervising Librarian at a large branch library in Bensonhurst where since 2003 he has led a philosophy discussion group for the public. In his spare time Dr. D'Angelo enjoys running, vegetarian cooking and reading. He would like to thank his friend and companion, Dr. Lisa J. Cohen, for her support.

Printed in the United States
80302LV00005B/45